EMERGING THREATS AND TECHNOLOGIES TO PROTECT THE HOMELAND

HEARING

BEFORE THE

SUBCOMMITTEE ON CYBERSECURITY, INFRASTRUCTURE PROTECTION, AND SECURITY TECHNOLOGIES

OF THE

COMMITTEE ON HOMELAND SECURITY HOUSE OF REPRESENTATIVES

ONE HUNDRED FOURTEENTH CONGRESS

FIRST SESSION

FEBRUARY 12, 2015

Serial No. 114–3

Printed for the use of the Committee on Homeland Security

Available via the World Wide Web: http://www.gpo.gov/fdsys/

U.S. GOVERNMENT PUBLISHING OFFICE

94–107 PDF   WASHINGTON : 2015

For sale by the Superintendent of Documents, U.S. Government Publishing Office
Internet: bookstore.gpo.gov   Phone: toll free (866) 512–1800; DC area (202) 512–1800
Fax: (202) 512–2104   Mail: Stop IDCC, Washington, DC 20402–0001

CONTENTS

EMERGING THREATS AND TECHNOLOGIES TO PROTECT THE HOMELAND

Thursday, February 12, 2015

U.S. HOUSE OF REPRESENTATIVES,
COMMITTEE ON HOMELAND SECURITY,
SUBCOMMITTEE ON CYBERSECURITY, INFRASTRUCTURE
PROTECTION, AND SECURITY TECHNOLOGIES,
Washington, DC.

The subcommittee met, pursuant to call, at 2:37 p.m., in Room 311, Cannon House Office Building, Hon. John Ratcliffe [Chairman of the subcommittee] presiding.

Present: Representatives Ratcliffe, Palazzo, Clawson, Richmond, Langevin, and Thompson.

Mr. RATCLIFFE. The Subcommittee on Cybersecurity, Infrastructure Protection, and Security Technologies will come to order.

The subcommittee meets today to exam critically important components within the Department of Homeland Security and to provide each of them an opportunity to give Members an update on the current state of affairs and direction moving forward, which will help inform this subcommittee's future oversight and legislative efforts.

Given the recent alarming terrorist attacks in Paris, the increase in violent extremist activity across Europe, and the increase in cyber attacks from nation-state and organized criminal actors, it is important that each of these components rise to the challenge and meet these threats.

Yesterday, the full committee heard from both the law enforcement and intelligence communities about the rising threat of foreign fighters and the risk from individuals who have traveled and trained with ISIS or other extremist groups in Syria and Iraq.

The National Protection and Programs Directorate is charged with the protection of our Nation's critical infrastructure in both the cyber and physical security realms. Cyber attacks and breaches against our Government agencies and critical infrastructure have grown exponentially, and the capabilities of our adversaries are becoming more advanced. As we have seen over the past few months with the hack of Sony Pictures and last week's breach of health insurance giant Anthem, these attacks are becoming the norm, and they are increasing in their sophistication.

The National Cybersecurity Communications and Integration Center, or NCCIC, within the NPPD is the leading the effort to prevent, detect, and mitigate cyber attacks against critical infrastructure, Federal agencies, and the private sector. The NCCIC's

(1)

mission is a critical civilian component in the sharing of threat information between the Government and the private sector.

The United States Secret Service also plays an important role in the sharing of cyber threat information through the NCCIC and back out to the private sector to help prevent and mitigate future attacks. The Secret Service Criminal Investigation Division investigates cyber crime cases involving financial breaches, such as the Target and Home Depot intrusions. The Secret Service also trains hundreds of State and local law enforcement officers, prosecutors, and judges in the field of computer forensics and digital evidence-handling techniques through its National Computer Forensics Institute.

The Domestic Nuclear Detection Office within DHS is responsible for detecting and deterring illicit nuclear and radiological material from entering the United States. While DNDO is the lead agency within the United States Government for coordinating these efforts, it works hand-in-hand with other DHS components, including TSA, Customs and Border Protection, State and local law enforcement, and the intelligence community. DNDO works with these partners to provide them with the technology, training, and best practices to ensure the interdiction of radiological or nuclear material before it can enter the United States.

While DNDO had previously experienced some stumbles along the way, under the current leadership of Dr. Gowadia it has become one of the best-functioning components within the Department of Homeland Security.

DNDO also works closely with the Science and Technology Directorate to further its mission. S&T is the primary research and development arm of DHS, and it manages science and technology research, development, and acquisition for the Department's operational components and first responders.

S&T has also experienced difficulties since its creation, some of which it is still grappling with today. These have included poor outreach efforts, inconsistent coordination with other DHS components, and a lack of clear research and development definitions. I know that S&T's director, Dr. Reginald Brothers, has been working to correct some of these issues over the past year, but it does concern me that some of these more basic issues have yet to be corrected. I am very much looking forward to working with Dr. Brothers and his staff to move the directorate forward.

I look forward to hearing from each of you that are here on today's panel about the current state of affairs and the anticipated future direction of each of your vital components. I am certain that Ranking Member Richmond and the other Members of the subcommittee also look forward to working with you and providing oversight and legislative solutions where appropriate.

[The statement of Chairman Ratcliffe follows:]

STATEMENT OF CHAIRMAN JOHN RATCLIFFE

FEBRUARY 12, 2015

The subcommittee meets today to examine critically important components within the Department of Homeland Security and to give each of them an opportunity to give Members an update on the current state of affairs and direction moving forward, which will help to inform this subcommittee's future oversight and legislative efforts.

Given the recent alarming terrorist attacks in Paris, the increase in radical and violent extremist activity across Europe and the increase in cyber attacks from nation-state and organized criminal actors, it's important that each of these components rise to the challenge and meet these threats. Yesterday, the full committee heard from the law enforcement and the intelligence communities about the rising threat of foreign fighters, and the risks from individuals who have traveled and trained with ISIS or other extremist groups in Syria and Iraq.

The National Protection and Programs Directorate is charged with the protection of our Nation's critical infrastructure in both the cyber and physical security realms. Cyber attacks and breaches against our Government agencies and critical infrastructure have grown exponentially, and the capabilities of our adversaries are becoming more advanced. As we have seen over the past few months with the hack of Sony Pictures, and last week's breach of health insurance giant Anthem, these attacks are becoming the norm and they're increasing in sophistication. The National Cybersecurity Communications and Integration Center within NPPD is leading the effort to prevent, detect, and mitigate cyber attacks against critical infrastructure, Federal agencies, and the private sector. The NCCIC's mission is a critical civilian component in the sharing of threat information between the Government and the private sector.

The United States Secret Service plays an important role in sharing of cyber threat information through the NCCIC and back out to the private sector to help prevent and mitigate future attacks. The Secret Service's Criminal Investigative Division investigates cybercrime cases involving financial breaches, such as the Target and Home Depot intrusions. The Secret Service also trains hundreds of State and local law enforcement officers, prosecutors, and judges in the field of computer forensics and digital evidence handling techniques through its National Computer Forensics Institute.

The Domestic Nuclear Detection Office within DHS is responsible for detecting and deterring illicit nuclear and radiological material from entering the United States. While DNDO is the lead agency within the United States Government for coordinating these efforts, it works hand-in-hand with other DHS components including TSA, Customs and Border Protection, State and local law enforcement and the intelligence community. DNDO works with these partners to provide them with the technology, training, and best practices to ensure the interdiction of radiological or nuclear material before it can enter the United States. While DNDO had previously experienced some stumbles along the way, under the current leadership of Dr. Gowadia, it has become one of the best functioning components within the Department.

DNDO also works closely with the Science and Technology Directorate to further its mission. S&T is the primary research and development arm of DHS, and it manages science and technology research, development, and acquisition for the Department's operational components and first responders. S&T has also experienced difficulties since its creation, some of which it is still grappling with today. These have included poor outreach efforts, inconsistent coordination with other DHS components, and a lack of clear research and development definitions. I know that S&T's director, Dr. Reggie Brothers, has been working to correct some of these issues over the past year but it does concern me that some of these more basic issues have yet to be corrected. I am very much looking forward to working with him and his staff to move the directorate forward.

I look forward to hearing from each of you on the current state of affairs and the anticipated future direction of each of your vital components. I'm certain that Ranking Member Richmond and the other Members of the subcommittee also look forward to working with you and providing oversight and legislative solutions where appropriate.

Mr. RATCLIFFE. The Chairman now recognizes the Ranking Minority Member of the subcommittee, the gentleman from Louisiana, Mr. Richmond, for any statement that he may have.

Mr. RICHMOND. Thank you, Mr. Chairman. Mr. Chairman, congratulations on assuming the Chair of this important subcommittee. Thank you for holding this hearing today on programs that are central to our oversight responsibilities.

I also want to thank the Ranking Member of the full committee, Mr. Thompson, for his participation in today's hearing and to highlight the tremendous level of expertise and experience that the Democrats bring to the subcommittee. In addition to the three most senior Democrats of the full committee, including Ranking Member Thompson, Ms. Sanchez, and Ms. Jackson Lee, we have a past Chairman of this subcommittee, Jim Langevin, who has returned to the committee after his term on Select Intelligence. Needless to say, we have a very strong team.

In the past, Chairs and Ranking Members of this subcommittee have found common ground on vital areas of policy that have helped protect our Nation's citizens and have been focused on protecting our critical infrastructure. I look forward to continuing this tradition of bipartisanship with Chairman Ratcliffe.

My primary focus will be to identify, oversee, and improve the authorities within DHS to help them assist our Nation's critical infrastructure to find acceptable and achievable levels of security from a wide range of man-made threats and natural disasters.

We know that the privately-owned entities that make up the Nation's critical infrastructure, including our ports, energy networks, chemical manufacturers, transportation and financial sectors, and telecommunication providers, are all vital to our societal and economic well-being.

Many constituents know all too well—my constituents know all too well what can happen when these systems fail. Ten years ago, the destruction of Hurricane Katrina had a debilitating impact on National security, economic security, and public health and safety. Needless to say, it is in the National interest to ensure that such critical infrastructure is adequately protected.

What we do here in Washington affects how firefighters, police, EMS technicians, border and maritime security, and doctors and nurses protect Americans every day, especially in times of disaster. Aside from the physical critical infrastructure security issues, both man-made and natural, it will be necessary to do all we can to develop a workable cyber protection framework for critical-infrastructure entities in order to protect the rest of our economy.

The President put forward a series of legislative proposals at the State of the Union that I think are a solid beginning for Congress to consider. These proposals would further refine and expand the authorities that DHS gained by last year's cybersecurity bills that were originated in and passed by this subcommittee and full committee, the Senate, and signed by the President.

In closing, I would be remiss if I did not mention the looming funding crisis at DHS. Although this crisis is mainly manufactured by my friends in the Majority, it is real nevertheless. Sixteen days from now, the bulk of DHS's management and support for the homeland security enterprise will be forced to close due to political gamesmanship.

We will hear testimony from the Congressional Research Service today that will outline the funding scenarios ahead of us and their likely impact on the programs that are being mentioned before us. I sincerely hope that we will all take heed to this sobering testimony and come together to find a solution.

Mr. Chairman, I look forward to working with you on the many complex challenges that face our subcommittee.

Thank you, and I yield back.

[The statement of Ranking Member Richmond follows:]

STATEMENT OF RANKING MEMBER CEDRIC L. RICHMOND

FEBRUARY 12, 2015

Mr. Chairman, congratulations on assuming the Chair of this important subcommittee, and thank you for holding this hearing today on programs that are central to our oversight responsibilities.

I also want to thank the Ranking Member of the full committee, Mr. Thompson, for his participation in today's hearing and to highlight the tremendous level of expertise and experience that the Democrats bring to the subcommittee.

In addition to the three most senior Democrats of the full committee including Ranking Member Thompson, Ms. Sanchez, and Ms. Jackson Lee, we have a past Chairman of this subcommittee, Jim Langevin who has returned to the committee after his term on Select Intelligence.

Needless to say, we have a very strong team.

In the past, Chairs and Ranking Members of this subcommittee have found common ground on vital areas of policy that have helped protect our Nation's citizens, and have been focused on protecting our critical infrastructure. I look forward to continuing that tradition of bipartisanship with Chairman Ratcliffe.

My primary focus will be to identify, oversee, and improve the authorities within DHS to help them assist our Nation's critical infrastructure to find acceptable and achievable levels of security from a wide range of man-made threats and natural disasters.

We know that the privately-owned entities that make up the Nation's critical infrastructure; including our ports, energy networks, chemical manufacturers, transportation and financial sectors, and telecommunication providers, are vital to our societal and economic well-being.

My constituents know all too well what can happen when these systems fail. Ten years ago, the destruction of Hurricane Katrina, had a debilitating impact on National security, economic security, and public health and safety. Needless to say, it is in the National interest to ensure that such critical infrastructure is adequately protected.

What we do here in Washington affects how firefighters, police, EMS technicians, border and maritime security, and doctors and nurses, protect Americans every day, especially in times of disaster.

Aside from the physical critical infrastructure security issues, both man-made and natural, it will be necessary to do all we can to develop a workable cyber protection framework for critical infrastructure entities in order to protect the rest of our economy.

The President put forward a series of legislative proposals at the State of the Union that I think are a solid beginning for Congress to consider. These proposals would further refine and expand the authorities that DHS gained by last year's cybersecurity bills that were originated in, and passed by this subcommittee and full committee, the Senate, and signed by the President.

In closing, I would be remiss if I did not mention the looming funding crisis at DHS. Although this crisis is mainly manufactured by my friends in the Majority, it is real nevertheless. Sixteen days from now, the bulk of DHS's management and support for the homeland security enterprise would be forced to close due to political gamesmanship.

We will hear testimony from the Congressional Research Service today that will outline the funding scenarios ahead of us, and their likely impact on the programs testifying before us. I sincerely hope that we all take heed to this sobering testimony and come together to find a solution.

Mr. Chairman, I look forward to working with you on the many complex challenges that face our subcommittee.

I yield back.

Mr. RATCLIFFE. I thank the gentlemen from Louisiana.

The Chairman now recognizes the Ranking Minority Member of the full committee, the gentleman from Mississippi, Mr. Thompson, for any statement that he may have.

Mr. THOMPSON. Thank you very much. Likewise, Mr. Chairman, welcome. I have been where you are. There is nothing like being in charge, trust me.

I am happy to have our witnesses here today.

Also, thank you for holding this hearing to discuss the developments and activities in the National Protection and Program Directorate, the Domestic Nuclear Detection Office, and the Science and Technology Directorate, all of which are important areas of oversight for this subcommittee.

I note that we are also to hear testimony today from the Cyber Operations Branch of the Secret Service. While I know this subcommittee has oversight of cybersecurity issues, Chairman McCaul and I agreed in the committee oversight plan for the 114th to include oversight of the Secret Service under the jurisdiction of the Subcommittee on Oversight and Management Efficiency.

While I am sure we will find the testimony interesting, I find it odd that the Service is testifying before a subcommittee that does not have oversight responsibilities, considering the difficulties the Service has experienced lately and the intense scrutiny the Service is under at this moment and especially in light of the recent shakeup in senior leadership, some of which occurred just a few days ago.

On another matter, if there is no quick resolution to the budget impasse regarding the continuing resolution in fiscal year 2015 appropriations, there are only 16 calendar days and 5 legislative days until the Department of Homeland Security shuts down on February 28, closing down the bulk of DHS's management and support of the homeland security infrastructure that was built following the 9/11 terrorist attack.

I will just mention a few of those things that would be impacted: Shuttering the DHS Domestic Nuclear Detection Office, which would no longer alert and coordinate with law enforcement agencies and withholding the Securing the Cities grants that pay for the critical nuclear detection capabilities in cities across the country; halting research and development work on countermeasures to devastating biological threats on nuclear detection equipment and on cargo and passenger screening technology; also crippling FEMA's preparation for future disasters and furloughing 22 percent of FEMA's personnel, as well as ending FEMA's training activities of local law enforcement for weapons-of-mass-destruction events.

Also, Mr. Chairman, some of DHS's employees would continue to work in the event of a shutdown. They would be forced to do so without pay, creating a significant distraction and dealing a tremendous blow to a Department with already low morale.

Among those who would be expected to protect Americans without getting paid would be more than 40,000 Border Patrol Agents and Customs and Border Patrol Officers; more than 50,000 TSA aviation security screeners; more than 13,000 Immigration and Customs Enforcement agents, more than 40,000 Active Duty Coast Guard military members; and more than 4,000 Secret Service law enforcement agents and officers.

With such serious consequences, it is no wonder three former DHS Secretaries sent a letter to Senators Mitch McConnell and Harry Reid calling for a clean DHS funding bill. The essential funding for the Department of Homeland Security is no place for the majority to showboat against immigration reform that strengthens our economy and our country.

Thank you, Mr. Chairman. With that, I yield back.

[The statement of Ranking Member Thompson follows:]

STATEMENT OF RANKING MEMBER BENNIE G. THOMPSON

FEBRUARY 12, 2015

Mr. Chairman, welcome to the gavel, and thank you for holding this hearing to discuss developments and activities in the National Protection and Program Directorate, the Domestic Nuclear Detection Office, and the Science and Technology Directorate, all of which are important areas of oversight for this subcommittee.

I note that we are also to hear testimony today from the cyber operations branch of the Secret Service. While I know this subcommittee has oversight on cybersecurity issues, Chairman McCaul and I agreed in the Committee Oversight Plan for the 114th to include oversight of the Secret Service under the jurisdiction of the Subcommittee for Oversight and Management Efficiency.

While I am sure we will find the testimony interesting, I find it odd that the Service is testifying before a subcommittee that does not have oversight responsibilities, considering the difficulties the Service has experienced lately and the intense scrutiny the Service is under at the moment, and especially in light of the recent shake-up in senior leadership, some of which occurred just a few days ago.

On another matter, if there is no quick resolution to the budget impasse regarding the Continuing Resolution and Fiscal Year 2015 Appropriations, there are only 16 calendar days and 5 legislative days until the Department of Homeland Security shuts down on February 28, closing down the bulk of DHS's management and support of the homeland security infrastructure that was built following the 9/11 terrorist attacks.

I will just mention a few:

- Shuttering the DHS Domestic Nuclear Detection Office, which would no longer alert and coordinate with local law enforcement agencies, and withholding the Securing the Cities grants that pay for critical nuclear detection capabilities in cities across the country;
- Halting Research and Development work on countermeasures to devastating biological threats, on nuclear detection equipment, and on cargo and passenger screening technologies;
- Crippling FEMA's preparations for future disasters, and furloughing 22 percent of FEMA personnel;
- Ending FEMA training activities with local law enforcement for Weapons of Mass Destruction events.

Although some DHS employees would continue to work in the event of a shutdown, they would be forced to do so without pay, creating a significant distraction and dealing a tremendous blow to a Department with already low morale.

Among those who would be expected to protect Americans without getting paid would be:

- More than 40,000 Border Patrol Agents and Customs and Border Patrol Officers;
- More than 50,000 TSA aviation security screeners;
- More than 13,000 Immigration and Customs Enforcement law enforcement agents and officers;
- More than 40,000 active-duty Coast Guard military members; and
- More than 4,000 Secret Service law enforcement agents and officers.

With such serious consequences, it is no wonder three former DHS Secretaries sent a letter to Senators Mitch McConnell and Harry Reid calling for a clean DHS funding bill. The essential funding for the Department of Homeland Security is no place for the Majority to showboat against immigration reform that strengthens our economy and our country.

Thank you, Mr. Chairman, and with that I yield back.

Mr. RATCLIFFE. I thank the gentleman from Mississippi.

Other Members of the subcommittee are reminded that opening statements may be submitted for the record.

We are pleased today to have a distinguished panel of witnesses before us on this very important topic.

I thank you all for being here.

I would like to recognize the panel en banc, and then each of you will have the opportunity to provide opening statements.

Our first witness is Mr. Andy Ozment. He is the assistant secretary for the Office of Cybersecurity and Communications within the National Protection and Programs Directorate of the Department of Homeland Security.

Welcome.

Our second witness, Dr. Huban Gowadia, is the director of the Domestic Nuclear Detection Office in the Department of Homeland Security.

Next, we will hear from Mr. Joseph Martin, who is the acting director of the Homeland Security Enterprise and First Responders Group within the Science and Technology Directorate at the Department of Homeland Security.

Also joining us today is Mr. William Noonan, who is the deputy special agent in charge of the Criminal Investigative Division at the United States Secret Service.

Finally, we have with us Mr. William Painter, a government and finance division analyst at the Congressional Research Service.

Again, the Chairman, the Ranking Member, and the Members of this subcommittee very much appreciate the witnesses' presence today.

The witnesses' full statements will appear in the record.

The Chairman now recognizes Mr. Ozment for 5 minutes to testify.

STATEMENT OF ANDY OZMENT, ASSISTANT SECRETARY, OF-FICE OF CYBERSECURITY AND COMMUNICATIONS, NA-TIONAL PROTECTION AND PROGRAMS DIRECTORATE, U.S. DEPARTMENT OF HOMELAND SECURITY

Mr. OZMENT. Thank you, Chairman.

Chairman Ratcliffe, Ranking Member Richmond, Ranking Member Thompson, and Members of the subcommittee, I am pleased to appear today to discuss the work of the Department of Homeland Security's National Protection and Programs Directorate, or NPPD, to address persistent and emerging cybersecurity risks to the U.S. homeland.

As the internet and network technologies become an increasingly omnipresent part of our daily lives, growing cyber threats present an increasing risk to critical infrastructure, our economy, and our National security.

As a Nation, we are faced with pervasive threats from malicious cyber actors. These individuals and groups are motivated by a variety of reasons that include espionage, political and ideological beliefs, and financial gain. For example, certain nation-states pose a significant economic cyber threat as they aggressively target and seek access to public- and private-sector computer networks with the goal of stealing and exploiting massive quantities of data, including intellectual property and other sensitive information. In another example, we saw in the recent Sony incident that cyber attacks also have the potential to damage physical infrastructure.

The DHS National Protection and Programs Directorate undertakes its cybersecurity activities within its overarching mission to secure and enhance the resilience of the Nation's cyber and physical infrastructure. We view ourselves as a customer service organization, and our customers are Federal civilian department and agencies, private-sector infrastructure owners and operators, and State, local, Tribal, and territorial governments.

In serving these customers, our guiding principles are to prioritize our customers' needs, to build and retain their trust, to ensure privacy and civil rights across the depth and breadth of our cyber and communications activities, and to enable continuous improvement to stay ahead of the malicious actors that we face.

To achieve our cybersecurity mission, we focus on helping our partners understand and manage cyber risk, reduce the frequency and impact of cyber incidents, and build partner capacity. So what do we bring to our customers? Broadly, we accomplish these goals through a variety of means, and I would like to highlight a few of them.

We share timely and accurate information and analysis to enable private and public-sector partners to protect themselves. We provide on-site assistance to Federal agencies and critical-infrastructure entities that are impacted by a significant cybersecurity incident. We provide technology and services to detect and block cyber threats from impacting Federal civilian agency networks.

We enable Federal agencies to more readily identify network security issues and take prioritized action. We provide Classified information to commercial cybersecurity companies so they can better protect their private-sector customers. And we maintain a trusted environment for private-sector partners to share information and collaborate to understand cybersecurity threats and trends.

These activities are only successful through our continued engagement and collaboration with public and private partners. NPPD engages its cybersecurity stakeholders through a variety of mechanisms, to include the National Cybersecurity and Communications Integration Center, or the NCCIC.

The NCCIC is a 24/7 National hub for sharing cyber and communications information between Federal agencies, the intelligence community, law enforcement, and the private sector. In 2014, the NCCIC received over 97,000 incident reports and issued nearly 12,000 actionable cyber alerts or warnings. NCCIC teams detected over 64,000 vulnerabilities on Federal and non-Federal systems and directly responded to 115 significant cyber incidents with on-site support to our customers.

Among its roles, the NCCIC provides incident response assistance during significant cyber events. The NCCIC also disseminates information on potential or active cybersecurity threats, incidents, and vulnerabilities to both public and private-sector partners. As a final example, the NCCIC conducts vulnerability assessments to identify cybersecurity risks and recommend mitigations.

Congress' support to these activities resulted in bipartisan action last year to pass critical cybersecurity legislation. That legislation enhanced our ability to measure and motivate Federal civilian agencies to improve their own security, it codified the NCCIC into law, and provides DHS with the ability to enhance our cyber workforce.

Enactment of these bills represents a significant moment for the Department's cybersecurity mission, and I thank Congress for this action. This committee, in particular, undertook significant efforts to bring these bills to enactment.

However, additional legislation is needed. Carefully updating laws to facilitate cybersecurity information sharing is essential to improving the Nation's cybersecurity. While many companies currently share cybersecurity threat information under existing laws, we need to increase the volume and speed of information shared between the Government and the private sector. It is essential to ensure that cyber threat information is shared quickly between trusted partners to detect and block cyber threats before they can cause damage.

The NCCIC's role is a critical piece of the President's recent legislative proposal because its core mission, as stated in this committee's unanimously passed National Cybersecurity Protection Act, is coordinating and serving as an interface for cybersecurity information across the Government and private sector. We must connect the dots, and the NCCIC is our mechanism for doing so.

Thank you for the opportunity to testify, and I look forward to any questions you may have.

[The prepared statement of Mr. Ozment follows:]

PREPARED STATEMENT OF ANDY OZMENT

FEBRUARY 12, 2015

INTRODUCTION

Chairman Ratcliffe, Ranking Member Richmond, and distinguished Members of the subcommittee, I am pleased to appear today to discuss the work of the Department of Homeland Security (DHS) to address persistent and emerging cyber threats to the U.S. homeland.

In my testimony today, I would like to highlight how DHS helps secure cyber infrastructure and discuss a few specific examples of instances in which we prevented and responded to a serious cybersecurity challenge.

THE ON-GOING CYBER THREAT

Growing cyber threats are an increasing risk to critical infrastructure, our economy and thus, our National security. As a Nation, we are faced with pervasive threats from malicious cyber actors. These individuals are motivated by a variety of reasons that include espionage, political and ideological beliefs, and financial gain. Certain nation-states pose a significant cyber threat as they aggressively target and seek access to public and private-sector computer networks with the goal of stealing and exploiting massive quantities of data.

Some nation-states consistently target Government networks for traditional espionage, theft of protected information for financial gain, and other purposes. Increasingly, State, local, Tribal, and territorial (SLTT) networks are experiencing nation-state cyber activity similar to that seen on Federal networks. In addition to targeting Government networks, there is a growing threat of nation-states targeting and compromising critical infrastructure networks and systems. Such attacks may provide persistent access for potential malicious cyber operations that could lead to cascading effects with physical implications, including injury or loss of life.

DHS CYBERSECURITY ROLE

The DHS National Protection and Programs Directorate (NPPD) undertakes its cybersecurity activities within its overarching mission to secure and enhance the resilience of the Nation's critical infrastructure. By leveraging its core capabilities of information and data sharing; incident response and capacity development; vulnerability assessments; and situational awareness, NPPD applies its expertise and resources to assist with building the Nation's resilience to physical and cybersecurity risks.

NPPD works with infrastructure owners and operators and Government partners, to provide timely information, analysis, and assessments through its field force and headquarters components. These capabilities are applied to maintain and provide situational awareness, increase resilience, and understand and mitigate risk. Through established partnerships including DHS support from partners in Science & Technology, U.S. Secret Service, and the Domestic Nuclear Detection Office, NPPD leads the National unity of effort for infrastructure security and resilience and builds the capacity of partners across the Nation. NPPD also directly protects Federal infrastructure against both physical and cyber threats and responds to incidents that threaten infrastructure or sensitive information.

NPPD executes this mission through several key responsibilities:

- *First, NPPD informs decision makers on potential impacts by performing comprehensive consequence analyses that assess cross-sector interdependencies and cascading effects.*—NPPD utilizes integrated analysis and modeling capabilities to understand cyber and physical risk and assist with prioritization of infrastructure to ensure resources are focused on protecting the assets or services of greatest significance. This capability also enables NPPD to maintain and provide situational awareness to public and private-sector partners about the potential impacts of future incidents and inform investments of various forms in effective preparedness given limited resources.

- *Second, NPPD reduces cyber and physical risks to critical infrastructure through collaboration with Federal agencies, State, local, Tribal, and territorial governments and the private sector.*—NPPD works with its partners to conduct voluntary critical infrastructure and cybersecurity assessments. These assessments allow partners to better understand their physical and cybersecurity resilience and vulnerabilities and provide recommendations for how they can improve. At the National level, NPPD leads or contributes to the development of risk management plans and approaches such as the National Infrastructure Protection Plan and the Cybersecurity Framework.

- *Third, NPPD programs promote cybersecurity knowledge and innovation to create a safer and more secure cyber environment.*—NPPD enables Federal departments and agencies to address cybersecurity challenges by providing guidance on technology, emerging risks, and best practices. To this end, NPPD partners with the private sector, law enforcement, military, and intelligence communities to identify and mitigate vulnerabilities and threats to information systems before they can cause significant harm.

- *Fourth, NPPD provides direct protection and conducts incident response activities to minimize the frequency and impact of incidents affecting Federal networks and facilities.*—NPPD secures and protects the buildings, grounds, and property owned or occupied by the Federal Government, as well as the people on those properties, by conducting Facility Security Assessments, recommending appropriate countermeasures, overseeing a large contract Protective Security Officer workforce, and exercising law enforcement authorities. On the cyber side, NPPD directly protects Federal networks by identifying vulnerabilities through the Continuous Diagnostics and Mitigation (CDM) program and by detecting and blocking threats through the EINSTEIN program. NPPD also responds to cyber incidents affecting Federal networks upon request of the impacted agencies to determine and recommend necessary mitigations.

- *Fifth, NPPD is responsible for ensuring effective telecommunications for Government users in National emergencies and for establishing policies and promoting solutions for interoperable emergency communications used on a daily basis across the country at the Federal, State, and local levels.*—As the Sector Specific Agency for Communications and for Emergency Services, NPPD protects and strengthens the security, reliability, survivability, and interoperability of the Nation's communications capabilities at the Federal, State, local, Tribal, and territorial levels. NPPD serves the first responder community by serving as a board member and providing technical assistance for the initiative to establish a National Public Safety Broadband Network and supports development of standards and best practices for the interoperability of first responder communications. NPPD is also helping lead the transition of public safety communications from land-mobile radio to broadband and Voice-Over-Internet Protocol (or VOIP). In order to ensure that communications are available to manage and coordinate a major incident, NPPD also assures the provision of National Security and Emergency Preparedness communications by administering the Priority Telecommunications Service (PTS).

DHS SHARES INFORMATION WIDELY WITH FEDERAL AGENCIES AND THE PRIVATE SECTOR, AND PROVIDES INCIDENT RESPONSE

DHS takes a customer-focused approach to information sharing, using information to detect and block cybersecurity attacks on Federal civilian agencies and sharing information to help critical infrastructure entities in their own protection. We provide information to commercial cybersecurity companies so they can better protect their customers through the Enhanced Cybersecurity Services program, or ECS, and we maintain a trusted information-sharing environment for private-sector partners to share information and collaborate on cybersecurity threats and trends via a program known as the Cyber Information Sharing and Collaboration Program, or CISCP. This trust derives in large part from our emphasis on privacy, confidentiality, civil rights, and civil liberties across all information-sharing programs, including special care to safeguard personally identifiable information.

DHS also maintains the National Cybersecurity & Communications Integration Center (NCCIC), which serves as a 24x7 centralized location for the coordination and integration of cyber situational awareness and incident management. NCCIC partners include all Federal departments and agencies; State, local, Tribal, and territorial governments; the private sector; and international entities. The NCCIC provides its partners with enhanced situational awareness of cybersecurity and communications incidents and risks, and provides timely information to manage vulnerabilities, threats, and incidents.

In 2014, the NCCIC received over 97,000 incident reports, and issued nearly 12,000 actionable cyber alerts or warnings. NCCIC teams also detected over 64,000 vulnerabilities on Federal and non-Federal systems and directly responded to 115 significant cyber incidents.

PROTECTING FEDERAL CIVILIAN CYBER INFRASTRUCTURE

DHS directly supports Federal civilian departments and agencies in developing capabilities that will improve their own cybersecurity posture. Through the Continuous Diagnostics and Mitigation (CDM) program, DHS enables Federal agencies to more readily identify network security issues, including unauthorized and unmanaged hardware and software; known vulnerabilities; weak configuration settings; and potential insider attacks. Agencies can then prioritize mitigation of these issues based upon potential consequences or likelihood of exploitation by adversaries. The CDM program provides diagnostic sensors, tools, and dashboards that provide situational awareness to individual agencies, and will provide DHS with summary data to understand relative and system risk across the Executive branch. NPPD is moving aggressively to implement CDM across all Federal civilian agencies. Memoranda of Agreement with the CDM program encompass over 97 percent of all Federal civilian personnel. An initial award of CDM tools in 2014 to fill immediate capability gaps at participating agencies, will, in the future, provide DHS with better data to protect the dot-gov, and has resulted in $26 million in cost avoidance. The President's 2016 budget requests $102.7 million for the CDM program. Two-thousand fifteen will be an exciting year for the CDM program: Acquisition Groups A and B, covering 7 agencies and over 45% of all Federal civilian personnel, will begin to deploy CDM tools starting in the third quarter of fiscal year 2015. By the first quarter of fiscal year 2016, 25 agencies and over 95% of all Federal civilian personnel will have started deploying CDM tools provided by DHS. NPPD is implementing a commercial off-the-shelf, or COTS, technology for the CDM dashboard to provide agencies with a detailed understanding of their cybersecurity risk and enable comprehensive situational awareness across the Federal Government. The agency-level dashboards will begin deployment in fiscal year 2015, and the Federal dashboard is expected to reach Full Operating Capability in fiscal year 2017.

While CDM will identify vulnerabilities and systemic risks within agency networks, the National Cybersecurity Protection System, or EINSTEIN, detects and blocks threats at the perimeter of the network or at the Internet Service Provider. EINSTEIN is an integrated intrusion detection, analysis, information sharing, and intrusion-prevention system. The President's 2016 budget requests $463.9 million for the EINSTEIN program. Perhaps the best way to understand EINSTEIN is through the analogy of a car attempting to enter a protected perimeter such as a military base. EINSTEIN 1 can be thought of as analogous to a cop on the beat looking for a particular license plate. The system captures key data about internet traffic entering an agency through basic network flow information. EINSTEIN 2 is akin to a cop who not only sees the license plate but sends an alert to other security personnel to alert them to a potentially prohibited or malicious vehicle. EINSTEIN 2's network intrusion detection system (IDS) technology uses custom signatures, based upon known or suspected cyber threats within Federal network traffic. EINSTEIN 3A, or E3A, is much like a gatehouse that prohibits vehicles whose license plates set off an alert from entering the base. E3A supplements EINSTEIN 2 by adding additional intrusion prevention capabilities and enabling ISPs, under the direction of DHS, to detect and block known or suspected cyber threats using indicators.

NPPD's Office of Cybersecurity and Communications (CS&C) screens all data captured by EINSTEIN 1 and EINSTEIN 2 sensors to ensure it is analytically relevant to a known or suspected cyber threat. E3A combines existing analysis of EINSTEIN 1 and EINSTEIN 2 data as well as information provided by cyber mission partners with existing commercial intrusion prevention security services to allow for the near-real-time deep packet inspection of Federal network traffic to identify and react to known or suspected cyber threats. Participating agencies currently have access to their network flow records through participation in EINSTEIN 1 and receive information about their own data specific to their networks in accordance with CS&C's cybersecurity information handling policies and guidelines. E3A is currently deployed and offering DNS and email services to eleven (11) departments and agencies, covering approximately 25% of all dot-gov (.gov) traffic. Forty-six (46) agencies have signed Memorandum of Agreements (MOA) to participate in E3A services covering 90% of all Federal civilian traffic. It reduces threat vectors available to actors seeking to infiltrate, control, or harm Federal networks. We look forward to working with Congress to further clarify DHS's authority to deploy this protective technology to Federal civilian systems.

SECURING THE HOMELAND AGAINST PERSISTENT AND EMERGING CYBER THREATS

Cyber intrusions into critical infrastructure and Government networks can cause significant damage and be perpetrated by increasingly sophisticated actors. The complexity of emerging threat capabilities, the inextricable link between the physical and cyber domains, and the diversity of cyber actors present challenges to DHS and our customers.

Financial Sector Distributed Denial of Service (DDoS) Attacks

Cyber attacks on the U.S. financial sector are often discussed as an area of concern. There were increasingly powerful DDoS incidents impacting leading U.S. banking institutions in 2012 and 2013, and high-profile media coverage of financial sector cybersecurity challenges in 2014. US–CERT has a distinct role in responding to a DDoS: To disseminate victim and potential victim notifications to United States Federal Agencies, Critical Infrastructure Partners, International CERTs, and U.S.-based Internet Service Providers.

US–CERT has provided technical data and assistance, including identifying 600,000 DDoS-related IP addresses and supporting contextual information. This information helps financial institutions and their information technology security service providers improve defensive capabilities. In addition to sharing with relevant private-sector entities, US–CERT provided this information to over 120 international partners, many of whom contributed to our mitigation efforts. US–CERT, along with the U.S. Secret Service, FBI and other interagency partners, also deployed to affected entities on-site technical assistance, or "boots on the ground." US–CERT works with Federal civilian agencies to protect USG systems from becoming part of a botnet, since botnets are a tool that cyber criminals use to deflect attribution in DDoS attacks.

During these attacks, our partners in the DHS Office of Intelligence and Analysis, or I&A, provided long-term, consistent threat updates to the Department of Treasury and private-sector partners in the Financial Services Sector. I&A analysts presented sector-specific Unclassified briefings on the relevant threat intelligence, including at the annual Financial Services Information Sharing and Analysis Center (FS–ISAC) conference, alongside the Office of the National Counterintelligence Executive and the U.S. Secret Service. At the request of the Treasury and the Financial and Banking Information Infrastructure Committee (FBIIC), I&A analysts provided Classified briefings on the malicious cyber threat actors to cleared individuals and groups from several financial regulators, including the Federal Deposit Insurance Corporation (FDIC), Securities and Exchange Commission (SEC), and the Federal Reserve Board (FRB).

Point-of-Sale Compromises

On December 19, 2013, a major retailer publically announced it had experienced unauthorized access to payment card data from the retailer's U.S. stores. The information involved in this incident included customer names, credit and debit card numbers, and the cards' expiration dates and card verification value (CVV) security codes. The CVV security codes are 3- or 4-digit numbers that are usually on the back of the card. Separately, another retailer also reported a malware incident involving its Point of Sale (POS) system on January 11, 2014, that resulted in the apparent compromise of credit card and payment information.

In response to this activity, NCCIC/US–CERT analyzed malware identified by the Secret Service as well as other relevant technical data and used those findings, in part, to create two information-sharing products. The first product, which is publicly available and can be found on US–CERT's website, provides a non-technical overview of risks to Point-of-Sale systems, along with recommendations for how businesses and individuals can better protect themselves and mitigate their losses in the event an incident has already occurred. The second product provides more detailed technical analysis and mitigation recommendations, and has been securely shared with industry partners to enable their protection efforts. NCCIC's goal is always to share information as broadly as possible, including by producing products tailored to specific audiences.

These efforts ensured that actionable details associated with a major cyber incident were shared with the private-sector partners who needed the information in order to protect themselves and their customers quickly and accurately, while also providing individuals with practical recommendations for mitigating the risk associated with the compromise of their personal information. NCCIC especially benefited from close coordination with the private-sector Financial Services Information Sharing and Analysis Center during this response.

CYBERSECURITY LEGISLATION

Last year, Congress acted in a bipartisan manner to pass critical cybersecurity legislation that enhanced the ability of the Department of Homeland Security to work with the private sector and other Federal civilian departments in each of their own cybersecurity activities, and enhanced the Department's cyber workforce. Enactment of these bills represents a significant moment for the Department's cybersecurity mission, and I thank Congress for this action. This committee in particular undertook significant efforts to bring the bills to passage.

Additional legislation is needed. While many companies currently share cybersecurity threat information under existing laws, there is a heightening need to increase the volume and speed of such information sharing between the Government and the private sector—and among appropriate private-sector organizations—without sacrificing the trust of the American people or individual privacy, civil rights, or civil liberties. It is also essential that we ensure the integration of threat indicators to provide shared situational awareness. We must connect the dots. Carefully updating laws to facilitate cybersecurity information sharing is essential to improving the Nation's cybersecurity. We also must provide law enforcement additional tools to fight crime in the digital age, create a National Data Breach Reporting requirement, and further clarify DHS's authority to deploy protective technologies to Federal, Executive branch, civilian systems.

CONCLUSION

DHS will continue to work with our public and private partners to create and implement collaborative solutions to improve cybersecurity, focused on reducing frequency and impact of high-consequence cybersecurity incidents. We work around the clock to ensure that the peace and security of the American way of life will not be interrupted by malicious actors seeking to exploit our reliance on the internet and networked technologies. Each incarnation of the cyber threat has unique traits, and mitigation requires agility and layered security. Cybersecurity is a process of risk management in a time of constrained resources, and we must ensure that our efforts achieve maximize security as efficiently as possible while preserving privacy, civil rights, and civil liberties.

DHS represents an integral piece of the National effort to increase our collective cybersecurity, but we cannot achieve our mission without a foundation of voluntary partnerships with the critical infrastructure community, industry, and our Government partners. While securing cyberspace has been identified as a core DHS mission since the 2010 Quadrennial Homeland Security Review the Department's view of cybersecurity has evolved to include a more holistic emphasis on critical infrastructure which takes into account the convergence of cyber and physical risk.

DHS will continue to serve as the center of integration, information sharing, and collaborative analysis, at machine-speed wherever possible, of global cyber risks, trends, and incidents. Through our unique role in protecting civilian Government systems and helping the private sector protect themselves, DHS can correlate data from diverse sources, in an anonymized and secure manner, to maximize insights and inform effective risk mitigation. We are working to further mature the ability of NCCIC to receive information at machine speed, which will support emerging capabilities of networks to self-heal and to recognize and block threats before they reach their targets. This will in turn diminish the profit model for cyber adversaries and reduce our response time to a cyber incident from days or hours to seconds.

DHS provides the foundation of the U.S. Government's approach to securing and ensuring the resilience of civilian critical infrastructure and essential services. We look forward to continuing the conversation and continuing to serve the American goals of peace and stability, and we rely upon your continued support. Thank you for the opportunity to testify, and I look forward to any questions you may have.

Mr. RATCLIFFE. Thank you, Mr. Ozment.

The Chairman now recognizes Dr. Gowadia to testify.

STATEMENT OF HUBAN A. GOWADIA, DIRECTOR, DOMESTIC NUCLEAR DETECTION OFFICE, U.S. DEPARTMENT OF HOMELAND SECURITY

Ms. GOWADIA. Good afternoon, Chairman Ratcliffe, Ranking Member Richmond, and Ranking Member Thompson, distinguished Members of the subcommittee. It is a pleasure to be here with my colleagues from the Department of Homeland Security and the Congressional Research Service to testify about the Domestic Nuclear Detection Office, or DNDO, on our on-going efforts to protect the homeland from nuclear and radiological threats.

As articulated in the new National security strategy, no threat poses as grave a danger to our security and well-being as the potential use of nuclear weapons and materials by irresponsible states or terrorists. DNDO was created in 2005 as an interagency with a singular focus—preventing nuclear terrorism—realized through two missions: Technical nuclear forensics and nuclear detection. We work with Federal, State, local, and international partners, as well as those in the private sector, academia, and the National laboratories.

For both missions, we are responsible for coordinating interagency efforts to develop strategies, conduct research, and deploy capabilities in support of our operational stakeholders. For example, DNDO's National Technical Nuclear Forensics Center provides centralized stewardship, planning, and integration of U.S. Government-wide efforts. Since the Center's establishment in 2006, DNDO has advanced nuclear forensics capabilities and improved National exercises by making them increasingly collaborative and realistic.

Focusing on an in extremis National capability, we are investing in our technical expertise pipeline. DNDO is on track to have 35 new Ph.D.'s added to the workforce by 2018.

On the detection mission, DNDO coordinates the United States Government's capabilities through the construct of the Global Nuclear Detection Architecture, or GNDA. Recently, in collaboration with our interagency partners, we published the 2014 GNDA Strategic Plan, which will guide our efforts as we collectively design and implement the architecture.

To address technical challenges, DNDO conducts an aggressive program of transformational research and development. Among our many accomplishments have been breakthrough sensing materials that have transitioned from the laboratory to commercially-available products. In fact, until recently, one such material, Stilbene, was only available in limited supplies from suppliers in Ukraine. Through our small-business innovation research efforts, U.S. industry now produces this material domestically at lower cost and in greater quantities.

As the Department's lead for acquiring and deploying radiation-detection systems, DNDO brings a rigorous and disciplined approach to testing and procurement. Since inception and in conjunction with our partners, we have completed over 100 test campaigns and 7 pilots to evaluate the performance of various nuclear detectors.

DNDO's collaborative systems acquisition efforts have ensured that all Coast Guard boarding parties and all TSA Viper teams are equipped with radiation detectors. All incoming general aviation flights are met by detector-equipped Customs and Border Protection officers. One hundred percent of trucks and cars and almost 100 percent of maritime containerized cargo is scanned for radiation at our ports of entry before release into the United States.

Because detection is about more than just equipment, we focus on the critical triad of intelligence, law enforcement, and technology. The ability to detect and interdict nuclear threats is maximized when well-trained law enforcement and public safety personnel conduct intelligence or information-driven operations using the right technology. Indeed, by the end of this year and working with our State and local partners, we intend to have basic preventive nuclear capabilities in all 50 States.

I would like to relate an excellent example of this triad at work. Last month, in Fairfield, Connecticut, a police officer stopped a stolen car and discovered an industrial radioactive source in the trunk. The officer contacted the local fire department and the Connecticut State Police Emergency Services Unit. Within 4 minutes, a trooper responded, equipped with radiation detectors provided via our Securing the Cities program. I should note that our S&T's National Urban Security Technology Laboratory supports this program.

The officers were thereby able to quickly resolve the situation at the local level using the right technologies and protocols. Information, law enforcement, and technology coming together to address radioactive material that was out of regulatory control.

In conclusion, DNDO has made considerable progress since its creation in 2005. As I have shared today, we are realizing the results of our research and development investments through the maturation of our Nation's nuclear detection and technical forensics capabilities. With your continued support, we will work steadfastly to make nuclear terrorism a prohibitively difficult undertaking for our adversaries.

Thank you for this opportunity, and I look forward to your questions.

[The prepared statement of Ms. Gowadia follows:]

PREPARED STATEMENT OF HUBAN A. GOWADIA

FEBRUARY 12, 2015

Chairman Ratcliffe, Ranking Member Richmond, and distinguished Members of the subcommittee. Thank you for the opportunity to testify before you today. I am honored to join my esteemed colleagues from the U.S. Department of Homeland Security (DHS) at this hearing regarding the emerging threats we face and the development of technologies employed to defend the homeland. Whether it is strengthening cybersecurity, combating cyber crime, protecting critical infrastructure, or preventing nuclear and radiological terrorism, DHS seeks to employ our Nation's talents and technological edge to defeat sophisticated and agile adversaries. I appreciate your attention to the threat of nuclear terrorism and your interest in the efforts and progress DHS' Domestic Nuclear Detection Office (DNDO) has made to prevent its occurrence.

As President Obama stated on March 25, 2014 at the joint press conference following the 2014 Nuclear Security Summit, "I convened the first Nuclear Security Summit in Washington four years ago because I believed that we need a serious and sustained global effort to deal with one of the greatest threats to international security—and that's the specter of nuclear terrorism . . . given the catastrophic consequences of even a single attack, we cannot be complacent." The potentially catastrophic effects of a nuclear detonation, whether executed surreptitiously by a state or a non-state actor, would have far-reaching impacts on our Nation and the world. A radiological attack, via a "dirty bomb," would result in far less destruction, but would still be extremely disruptive to our way of life.

The spectrum of nuclear security spans physical protection of nuclear and other radioactive materials, detection of such materials out of regulatory control, rendering devices safe, response and recovery to incidents, and forensics and attribution of materials. DNDO has specific, focused responsibilities for two elements in this spectrum: Detection and nuclear forensics. And as reducing the risk of nuclear terrorism is a whole-of-Government challenge, DNDO works with Federal, State, local, Tribal, territorial, and international partners as well as those in the private sector, academia, and the National laboratories to fulfill its mission.

AUTHORITIES

With the recognition of the need to focus efforts to detect nuclear and other radioactive materials that have become unsecured, DNDO was established in 2005 by National Security Presidential Directive (NSPD)–43 and Homeland Security Presidential Directive (HSPD)–14 and subsequently codified in Title V of the Security and Accountability For Every (SAFE) Port Act (Pub. L. No. 109–347), which amended the Homeland Security Act of 2002. Pursuant to section 1902 of the Homeland Security Act, DNDO is required to develop, with the approval of the Secretary and in coordination with the Departments of Energy (DOE), State (DOS), Defense (DoD), and Justice (DOJ), an enhanced global nuclear detection architecture (GNDA), and is responsible for implementing the domestic portion.

The architecture serves as a framework for detecting (through technical and nontechnical means), analyzing, and reporting on nuclear and other radioactive materials that are out of regulatory control. Non-technical detection refers to an alert from law enforcement or intelligence efforts and collected by GNDA partners under their statutory authorities and consistent with National policy. DNDO is also charged to enhance and coordinate the nuclear detection efforts of Federal, State, local, and Tribal governments and the private sector to ensure a managed, coordinated response. To accomplish this, DNDO leads programs to conduct transformational research and development for advanced detection technologies, deploy nuclear detection capabilities, measure detector system performance, and ensure effective response to detection alarms.

In 2006, DNDO's National Technical Nuclear Forensics Center was established by NSPD–17/HSPD–4 and later authorized by the 2010 Nuclear Forensics and Attribution Act (Pub. L. No. 111–140) with the mission of characterizing radiological and nuclear devices prior to detonation. DNDO was given responsibilities to provide centralized stewardship, planning, and integration for all Federal nuclear forensics activities. The Act also established the National Nuclear Forensics Expertise Development program and required DNDO to lead the development and implementation of the National Strategic Five-Year Plan for Improving the Nuclear Forensics and Attribution Capabilities of the United States.

These authorities have directed our focus in preventing nuclear terrorism through the enhancement of nuclear detection and technical forensics capabilities. In both instances, we rely on the critical triad of intelligence, law enforcement, and technology. Thus, to maximize the Nation's ability to detect and interdict a threat, it is imperative that we apply detection technologies in operations that are driven by intelligence indicators, and place them in the hands of well-trained law enforcement and public safety officials. Similarly, to enhance attribution capabilities, the U.S. Government (USG) must ensure that information from law enforcement, intelligence, and technical nuclear forensics is synthesized to identify the origin of the material or device and the perpetrators.

While we have made significant improvements in both detection and forensics over the years, the threat of nuclear terrorism persists, and requires constant vigilance.

DEVELOPING THE GLOBAL NUCLEAR DETECTION ARCHITECTURE

Cited in Presidential Directive and legislation, the GNDA is a multi-faceted, layered, defense-in-depth framework, with the objective of making the illicit acquisition, fabrication, and transport of a nuclear or radiological device or material prohibitively difficult. DNDO relies on a well-conceived arrangement of fixed and mobile radiological and nuclear technical detection capabilities to present terrorists with many obstacles to a successful attack, including greatly increasing costs, difficulty, and risk.

To develop the architecture, DNDO assesses current and planned capabilities against the evolving radiological and nuclear threat, using rigorous risk assessments, for example. Since 2007, and as directed by HSPD–18 (Medical Countermeasures against Weapons of Mass Destruction), DNDO has collaborated with the DHS Science & Technology Directorate (S&T) to produce the Integrated Chemical, Biological, Radiological, and Nuclear Terrorism Risk Assessment. DNDO leads the biennial radiological and nuclear terrorism risk assessment, which is then combined with similar biological and chemical risk assessments. In order to better inform resource allocation decisions, DNDO has improved the threat models in the risk assessment by adding an adaptive, intelligent adversary model and is working with DOE's National Laboratories to enhance improvised nuclear device models. DNDO has also supported DHS risk assessments such as the Strategic National Risk Assessment and the Homeland Security National Risk Characterization. DNDO is also working with operational partners to develop models that will provide vulnerability estimates for the risk assessment and more refined estimates for impacts to operations.

To guide the strategic direction of the GNDA, the USG interagency developed the first-ever Global Nuclear Detection Architecture Strategic Plan in December 2010. In April 2012, the Secretary of Homeland Security issued a DHS Global Nuclear Detection Architecture Implementation Plan, which identified priorities, necessary capabilities, and monitoring mechanisms to assess progress. Recently, DNDO has worked with interagency partners to update the Global Nuclear Detection Architecture Strategic Plan. The 2014 Strategic Plan presents an updated definition and vision for the GNDA, as well as a mission, goals, and objectives for interagency efforts to detect, analyze, and report on nuclear or other radioactive materials that are out of regulatory control.

While USG efforts and programs are critical, developing a global nuclear detection architecture relies largely on the decisions of sovereign foreign partners to develop and enhance their own national and regional detection programs. DNDO contributes to interagency efforts led by the Department of State by laying the groundwork to assist partner nations in developing defense-in-depth approaches to detecting illicitly trafficked nuclear or other radioactive materials. DNDO has also assisted in the development of guidelines and best practices through the Global Initiative to Combat Nuclear Terrorism and the International Atomic Energy Agency (IAEA) to outline the key characteristics of an effective architecture. To date, IAEA has used these guidelines and best practices in six regional training courses to help 42 nations initiate planning of national-level detection architectures, with over 100 planners trained in architecture development. To make the course available to a broad set of stakeholders, DNDO assisted the IAEA in conducting a train-the-trainer session to further expand the instructor pool to allow for English, Spanish, and French language versions of the course. This strategic partnership will continue to serve as a force multiplier for USG nuclear security efforts for years to come.

CONDUCTING TRANSFORMATIONAL RESEARCH AND DEVELOPING SYSTEMS

Pursuant to Presidential Directive and the law, DNDO is also responsible for conducting an aggressive, evolutionary, and transformational program of research and development to generate and improve technologies to detect nuclear and radioactive materials. DNDO's transformational research and development efforts seek to achieve dramatic advancements in technologies to enhance our National detection and forensics capabilities. These developments may also reduce the cost and operational burden of using advanced technology in the field to maintain an enhanced level of protection. Annually, DNDO updates its research and development strategy based on prevailing risk, advancements in technology, and the availability of funding. By supporting technological advancement for both nuclear detection and forensics, DNDO achieves a strategic and fiscal benefit for the Government.

Although significant progress has been made in addressing the gaps and needs of the GNDA and nuclear forensics, several challenges remain that require sustained investment. DNDO's technical challenges include the need for systems that:

- Are cost-effective with sufficient technical performance to ensure wide-spread deployment;
- Can detect special nuclear material, such as plutonium and uranium, even when heavily shielded;
- Facilitate enhanced wide-area searches in a variety of scenarios, to include urban and highly cluttered environments;
- Can be used to monitor traffic in challenging pathways, such as between ports of entry along our land and sea borders; and
- Determine the origin and manufacturing process of seized material.

DNDO has and will continue to advance fundamental knowledge in nuclear detection and forensics through a sustained long-term investment in the Exploratory Research program and Academic Research Initiative. These efforts directly address the aforementioned challenges through basic and applied research to feed more mature research and development projects such as DNDO's Advanced Technology Demonstrations.

To develop essential technical expertise while advancing fundamental knowledge in nuclear sciences, DNDO invests in academic research through the Academic Research Initiative, supporting the next generation of scientists and engineers in areas such as advanced materials, nuclear engineering, radiochemistry, and deterrence theory. Since inception in 2007, DNDO has awarded 77 grants to 50 academic institutions, and supported over 400 students. On average, this program support results in over 50 journal papers per year. We are beginning to see these projects move up the technology pipeline. A new room temperature thallium-based semiconductor detector was transferred from Northwestern University to our Exploratory Research program and is now in its preliminary design review phase of development. Nuclear resonance cross-sections measured at Duke University are being used in our shielded special nuclear material detection projects, and background radiation measurements performed by University of California at Berkeley are being used in support of programs across the interagency.

Several DNDO-sponsored research efforts have also led to new commercial products that provide enhanced operational capabilities to Federal, State, and local law enforcement and public safety personnel. Even before a Helium-3 shortage was identified, DNDO teamed with the Defense Threat Reduction Agency to explore options for better, more cost-effective alternatives for neutron detection.[1] For portal systems, which require the largest quantities of this gas, DNDO worked with industry and is now deploying alternative detection technologies that do not require Helium-3. This enables the country to devote the scarce supplies of Helium-3 to those applications where no substitutes are possible. We have tested Helium-3 alternative technologies for use in mobile, backpack, and hand-held radiation detectors, several of which have already shown performance superior to the current-generation technologies. Importantly, due to a collaborative USG-wide effort to address the shortfall, our USG strategic reserve of Helium-3 can meet demand beyond fiscal year 2040.

Other recent DNDO technological successes that transitioned from laboratories to commercially-available products include:
- Advanced radiation sensing materials such as cesium lithium yttrium chloride, strontium iodide, and stilbene, which have enhanced detection characteristics and can be used to build more capable systems featuring simplified electronics, low power requirements, and greater reliability;
- New electronics and advanced algorithms, for data processing for identifying radioisotopes that support networked radiation detection for improved wide-area search capabilities;
- Compact dual-energy X-ray generators with improved density discrimination and higher shielding penetration that have been integrated into commercially-available mobile radiography systems; and
- Software to automatically detect special nuclear material and shielding material in radiography images.

DNDO continues to develop breakthrough technologies that increase performance and reduce the operational burdens of our front-line operators and improve their mission performance. For example, we are collaborating with U.S. Customs and Border Protection's (CBP) Laboratories and Scientific Services to use machine learning to greatly reduce the number of nuisance alarms in radiation portal monitors. In addition, we work with the Massachusetts Port Authority, S&T's Border and Maritime Security Division, and the United Kingdom's Home Office to develop and evalu-

---

[1] Helium-3 is a gas that is widely used to detect neutrons that are emitted by certain nuclear and other radioactive materials. Helium-3 results from the radioactive decay of tritium. As the need for tritium for nuclear weapons decreased, so too did the availability of Helium-3.

ate the next generation non-intrusive inspection imaging equipment. Of particular note, the collaboration in this case is expected to produce the first wholly-integrated system capable of detecting both nuclear material and contraband. Further, we jointly evaluate parameter-setting modifications to reduce the number of alarms from naturally-occurring radioactive material. In fact, after a rigorous program of laboratory tests, modeling and simulation, field trials, and successful pilots at two ports of entry, CBP has deployed the new technique to 26 seaports and 7 land border crossings through January 2015. This technique, which involves adjustments to the settings on the radiation portal monitors, is yielding operational efficiencies by reducing alarm rates from benign sources and the associated time CBP Officers would have needed to manually inspect that cargo.

In addition to CBP, DNDO worked closely with the U.S. Coast Guard (USCG), the Transportation Security Administration (TSA), and State and local partners to identify key operational requirements for the design of next-generation radioisotope identification devices that can be used by law enforcement officers and technical experts during routine operations to identify radioactive materials and adjudicate alarms. Based on the enhanced detection material lanthanum bromide and improved algorithms, this new hand-held technology is easy-to-use, lightweight, and more reliable and, because it contains built-in calibration and diagnostics, has a much lower annual maintenance cost. An example of a successful acquisition program, the new system is receiving very positive reviews from operators in the field.

CHARACTERIZING SYSTEM PERFORMANCE

DNDO's technology development efforts are coupled with a rigorous test and evaluation program. Over the years, DNDO's test program has grown and matured. To date, we have conducted more than 100 test and evaluation campaigns at more than 40 laboratory and operational venues, and evaluated systems including pagers, handhelds, portals, backpacks, and vehicle-, boat-, aircraft,- and crane-mounted detectors, as well as next-generation radiography technologies. To ensure the equipment is evaluated in the manner in which it will be used, these test campaigns are always planned and executed with operational users. In addition, we include interagency partners and use peer-reviewed processes. The results from DNDO's test campaigns have informed Federal, State, local, and Tribal partners on the technical and operational performance of detection systems, allowing them to select the most suitable equipment and implement the most effective concepts of operation for their unique needs.

Pursuant to the law, DNDO leads the development of technical capability standards, and in collaboration with the National Institute of Standards and Technology, also supports the development, publication, and adoption of National consensus standards for radiation detection equipment. A total of 24 standards, including 11 U.S. standards with the American National Standards Institute, 10 international standards with the International Electrotechnical Commission, and 3 technical capability standards now exist for homeland security applications. We have assessed commercially-available detection systems against National and international standards and in various operational scenarios. Notably, we completed the Illicit Trafficking Radiation Assessment program, a collaboration with the European Commission's Joint Research Center and the IAEA to evaluate nearly 80 instruments against consensus standards. The results enabled our stakeholders to compare the performance of commercially-available radiation detection equipment and provided manufacturers with constructive feedback on their products.

IMPLEMENTING THE DOMESTIC COMPONENT OF THE GLOBAL NUCLEAR DETECTION ARCHITECTURE

DNDO is instrumental in implementing the domestic component of the global nuclear detection architecture. In conjunction with Federal, State, local, Tribal, and territorial operational partners, DNDO applies a disciplined approach to procure small and large-scale radiation detection and/or identification systems and deploy them at ports of entry, along our land and maritime borders, and in the interior of the United States. In addition, as part of DHS's Strategic Sourcing efforts, DNDO is the Department's commodity manager for hand-held radiological and nuclear detection equipment. This enables us to take advantage of technical advancements and achieve cost savings by leveraging the volume demand of Department-wide and other Federal users.

DNDO's collaborative system acquisition efforts have ensured that all USCG boarding parties have radiation detection equipment; all in-coming general aviation flights are met by CBP Officers with radiation detectors; 100 percent of trucks and cars entering our Nation at land ports of entry are scanned for nuclear and other radioactive materials; almost 100 percent of maritime containerized cargo is similarly scanned at our sea ports of entry; and the TSA's Visible Intermodal Prevention and Response teams are equipped with radiation detectors.

While technology acquisition and deployments are critical, we must also ensure that the training, exercise, and cross-jurisdictional protocols integral to mission success are adopted and sustained by operational partners. As such, DNDO provides program assistance services to Federal, State, local, Tribal, and territorial stakeholders who are developing or enhancing radiological and nuclear detection capabilities. This support includes assistance in developing and integrating local or regional programs into the global nuclear detection architecture, guiding the development of concepts of operations and standard operating procedures, and developing training and exercise products to ingrain those procedures into day-to-day activities.

DNDO has made considerable progress in enhancing National radiological and nuclear detection capabilities in the following ways:

- We are on schedule to complete discussions on the establishment, maintenance, and sustainment of radiological and nuclear detection programs in all 50 States by the end of 2015.
- In conjunction with regional partners, we have developed robust detection capability in the New York City region, through the Securing the Cities program, where more than 19,450 personnel have been trained in nuclear detection operations and more than 8,800 pieces of detection equipment have been deployed. National program implementation began with expansion to Los Angeles/Long Beach in 2012, and they are beginning to train personnel and receive detection equipment. In 2014, the National Capital Region was selected as the third Securing the Cities site.
- DNDO's Assistance Program is currently engaged with 33 States, two major Urban Area Security Initiative regions (non-Securing the Cities), and 28 U.S. Coast Guard Area Maritime Security Committees.
- Since 2008, DNDO has deployed Mobile Detection Deployment Units over 200 times to provide radiological and nuclear detection and communications equipment for Federal, State, and local agencies to augment their capabilities during special events or in response to elevated threat conditions.

DNDO provides training products and support to develop, enhance, and expand radiological and nuclear detection capabilities. In partnership with the Federal Emergency Management Agency (FEMA), the Federal Law Enforcement Training Center, DOE, and DOJ, DNDO develops and implements protocols and training standards for the effective use of radiation detection equipment and associated alarm reporting and resolution processes. Since 2006, DNDO has developed 49 training courses listed in the Federal course catalog. In collaboration with interagency partners, including the Federal Law Enforcement Training Center, more than 33,500 law enforcement personnel and public safety officials from 35 States have participated in DNDO-supported radiological and nuclear detection training.

DNDO also assists State and local partners in developing, designing, and conducting exercises that are compliant with the Homeland Security Exercise and Evaluation program methodology. The exercises provide valuable hands-on experience for personnel performing radiological and nuclear detection operations and assist decision makers in integrating the detection mission into their daily operations, while fostering the exchange of ideas and best practices amongst State and local partners. Since 2006, DNDO has conducted exercises with 21 States and annually supports up to 20 exercises. In fiscal year 2014, DNDO conducted 19 domestic exercises with State and local partners, as well as two international exercises.

DNDO fields a unique Red Team that can objectively assess the operational effectiveness and performance of DNDO programs and deployed radiological and nuclear detection capabilities at the Federal, State, and local levels. Our Red Team works across the interagency employing a whole-of-Government approach to improve our National capabilities. At the Federal level we partner with DoD, DOE, and DOJ; within DHS with CBP, FEMA, TSA, USCG, and U.S. Secret Service; and with a myriad of State and local agencies across the United States. The Red Team evaluates deployed systems and operations and their associated tactics, techniques, and procedures, in as-close-to-realistic environments as possible. As covert and overt assessments are generally the only opportunity for operators of radiological and nuclear detection systems to gain experience detecting uncommon nuclear sources, these operations provide valuable feedback on the performance of tactics, techniques, and procedures. This feedback enables operators to improve their concepts of operation and readiness. For the past 5 years, DNDO's Red Team has averaged more than 25 overt and covert assessments per year, successfully conducting 33 evaluations in fiscal year 2014 in support of operational partners.

DNDO is responsible for enhancing and coordinating the nuclear detection efforts of Federal, State, local, and Tribal governments and the private sector to ensure a managed, coordinated response. We also coordinate across the interagency to establish protocols and procedures to ensure that the technical detection of unauthorized nuclear explosive devices, fissile material, or other active radioactive material is promptly reported to the Secretaries of Homeland Security, Defense, and Energy, the Attorney General, and others as appropriate for action by law enforcement, military, emergency response, or other authorities.

DNDO's Joint Analysis Center is essential in enhancing situational awareness, as well as providing technical support and informational products, to Federal, State, and local partners. The Joint Analysis Center maintains and provides awareness for mission partners of deployed detection capabilities, monitoring on-going events or threats, and maintaining historical data. Using the Joint Analysis Center Collaborative Information System, DNDO facilitates nuclear alarm adjudication and the consolidation and sharing of information through geographic information system displays and databases. This system is available for direct access by our State and local partners, providing them with the ability to manage, document, and execute a radiological and nuclear detection program. This includes the ability to electronically maintain training and certification, and consolidates and maintains a database of detector equipment and Nuclear Regulatory Commission State licensees. Through this information system, we connect to the Triage system, maintained by DOE's National Nuclear Security Administration, to enable a seamless transition when National-level adjudication assistance is required. To increase awareness of lost and stolen sources and other relevant information, DNDO's Joint Analysis Center publishes Unclassified weekly information bulletins, summarizing relevant news articles and providing useful facts about radioactive materials. This weekly information bulletin currently reaches every DHS Fusion Center and over 2,000 global nuclear detection architecture stakeholders.

In addition to direct interaction with individual States and law enforcement agencies, DNDO hosts biannual State and Local Stakeholder Working Group meetings and Executive Steering Council meetings with law enforcement and other supervisory personnel to exchange best practices and to obtain feedback on DNDO's initiatives. The State and Local Stakeholder Working Group provides a forum for DNDO to meet with our stakeholders to discuss their current activities, lessons learned, and planned detection initiatives. This forum also provides State and local leaders an opportunity to convey their perspective on mission needs and radiation detection requirements, so that DNDO can develop the necessary products and services to support their efforts. The Executive Steering Council provides policy coordination and implementation between DNDO and senior-level State and local leaders regarding radiation detection programs, and serves as a mechanism to solicit input from senior leaders on their successes, evolving requirements and challenges, as well as for DNDO to apprise them of on-going efforts to support their jurisdictions. Both the Stakeholder Working Group and the Executive Steering Council have been received favorably and continue to reinforce the relationship between DNDO and key stakeholders.

ACQUISITION PROCESS IMPROVEMENTS

To enhance mission delivery and improve investment management, DNDO designed the Solution Development Process. Aligned with DHS Acquisition Management Directive 102–01, the Solution Development Process institutes an integrated governance approach to program and project oversight throughout the systems engineering life cycle. The process brings all programs and projects under leadership governance-establishing a shared language, with common practices to increase efficiencies, promote programmatic and budgetary transparency, and bolster accountability. It aligns with DHS enterprise architecture, acquisition management, and capital planning and investment processes. A critical component of the process is the active involvement of operational partners, who serve as Lead Business Authorities, and requires rigorous technical reviews at each programmatic stage. In adhering to the process, DNDO ensures current and future programs are appropriately structured and have the necessary oversight for success. DNDO will continue to incorporate lessons learned and process improvements as the process matures, sharing them throughout DHS to strengthen Departmental unity of effort—one of the Secretary's top priorities.

Based in part on lessons learned from the cancelled Advanced Spectroscopic Portal program, DNDO has significantly bolstered acquisition management policy and strengthened its implementation via robust and disciplined governance and program management processes. DNDO closely collaborated with CBP to complete a post-implementation review and identified 32 lessons learned, including findings in acquisition management. These efforts have enabled us to ensure that programs are selected based on sound business cases and are well-managed, resulting in an efficient and effective use of DNDO's appropriated funds.

Finally, recognizing the important contributions and innovations of private industry, National laboratories, and academia, DNDO has evolved its acquisition focus from one that is predominantly fueled by a Government-funded, Government-managed development process to one that relies upon industry-led research and development. As such, DNDO technology development programs now proceed with a "commercial first" approach; engaging first with the private sector for solutions and only moving to a Government-sponsored and managed development effort if necessary. This approach leverages private-sector innovation, taking advantage of industry's innate flexibility and ability to rapidly improve technologies. In some cases, shifting to commercial-based acquisitions will even reduce the total time to test, acquire, and field technology.

FORENSICS CAPABILITIES

An act of nuclear terrorism or an interdiction of a nuclear threat would necessitate rapid, accurate attribution. Any USG response would need sound scientific evidence supporting the determination of the responsible parties. Nuclear forensics would support leadership decisions. DNDO's National Technical Nuclear Forensics Center focuses on continuously evaluating and improving the nuclear forensics capabilities with specific responsibilities to:
- Improve the readiness of the overarching USG nuclear forensic capabilities, from pre- to post-detonation, through centralized stewardship, planning, assessment, exercises, improvement, and integration;
- Advance the technical capabilities of the USG to perform forensic analyses on pre-detonation nuclear and other radioactive materials; and
- Build and sustain an expertise pipeline for nuclear forensic scientists.

Operational readiness of USG nuclear forensics capabilities has improved markedly in recent years. Efforts of the nuclear forensics community are integrated through the alignment of program capabilities, coordination of research and development and operational activities, and accelerated capability development through synchronized interagency investments. The interagency uses two primary DNDO-led mechanisms, the Nuclear Forensics Executive Council and Steering Committee, to facilitate consistent coordination across the USG. DNDO led the interagency effort to update and extend the National Strategic Five-Year Plan for Improving the Nuclear Forensics and Attribution Capabilities of the United States, completing it in December 2014, and continues to synchronize resources among partner agencies through an established budget crosscut. Requirements are now regularly identified and developed by the Nuclear Forensics Requirements Center, co-chaired by DNDO and the FBI.

Since the Nuclear Security Summit in 2010, international partnerships in nuclear forensics have greatly expanded, resulting in stronger National and international capabilities. DNDO provides subject-matter expertise to numerous initiatives, including multinational nuclear forensics table-top exercises, to enhance understanding among policy makers, law enforcement officials, and scientists, and to encourage and assist other nations in developing their national capabilities.

Forensics exercises have become increasingly realistic and complex, with intensive multi-agency planning among the FBI, DOE, Army, Air Force, and DNDO. Many of the exercises now include State and local law enforcement. Other exercises have involved the Federal law enforcement and intelligence communities in order to plan and synchronize the fusion of intelligence, law enforcement, and technical forensics information, leading to a more efficient and effective attribution process. In the international context, DNDO was involved in the "@tomic 2014" table-top exercise in February of last year, bringing together 31 nations and several international organizations to enhance knowledge and awareness of how nuclear forensics can be used in nuclear smuggling cases. The exercise served as a side event leading up to and informing the Nuclear Security Summit 2014.

Technical nuclear forensics capabilities for analysis of nuclear and other radioactive materials have steadily advanced. DNDO's efforts are focused on continually improving the accuracy, precision, and timeliness of material characterization information, and linking that information to the process and place of that material's origin. To date, DNDO has developed seven radiological and nuclear certified reference materials, which are forensically-relevant calibration standards used by the National laboratories to improve confidence in analytical conclusions. Additionally, DNDO has developed the first-ever laboratory-scale uranium processing capability that allows us to determine forensic signatures associated with specific variations in uranium manufacturing processes. This capability enables us to determine forensics signatures without having direct access to samples from foreign fuel cycles. We are now developing a similar plutonium processing capability. Further, in cooperation with DOE and DoD, DNDO has developed and installed a nuclear forensics data evaluation capability at Sandia National Laboratories that enables forensic scientists to develop and test data analysis tools and evaluate large sets of data in order to identify distinguishing characteristics of specific nuclear materials. DNDO remains focused on advancing the National ability to trace nuclear materials back to their source.

DNDO's efforts to restore the National expertise pipeline have also shown substantial success to date. The Congressionally-mandated National Nuclear Forensics Expertise Development program is a comprehensive effort to grow and sustain the scientific expertise required to execute the National technical nuclear forensics mission. Launched in 2008, this effort is a key component in assuring a robust and enduring nuclear forensics capability and its contribution to the Nation's efforts at preventing nuclear terrorism. In close partnership with eight National Laboratories, the program has provided support to more than 300 students and faculty and 27 universities in partnership with 11 National laboratories. We are steadily progressing toward adding 35 new Ph.D. scientists to the nuclear forensics field by 2018 to revitalize the pipeline and replace anticipated attrition or retirements from the DOE National Laboratories. Twenty-four new nuclear forensics scientists have come through the National Nuclear Forensics Expertise Development program and been hired by the National laboratories and Federal agencies since the program's inception.

CLOSING

Thank you again for the opportunity to discuss the on-going efforts of DNDO to prevent and protect against radiological threats.

While DNDO has made considerable progress since it was established in 2005, much remains to be done. It will be a challenge to remain one step ahead of the adversary—particularly one that is intelligent and adaptable. We must ensure our efforts are robust so that the obstacles terrorists face are many. DNDO's detection and forensics programs, in concert with those of our partners and stakeholders, both in these areas and along the spectrum of nuclear security, are foundational elements in creating these impediments. Together, we can build upon DNDO's integrated approach to architecture planning, testing and assessments, research and development, operational support, and nuclear forensics to strengthen the Nation's capabilities to deter, detect, and interdict the nuclear threat and to hold those responsible accountable for their actions. We remain committed to this challenge and deeply appreciate this subcommittee's sustained interest and support in our shared goals to secure the homeland.

Mr. RATCLIFFE. Thank you, Dr. Gowadia.

The Chairman now recognizes Mr. Martin for his testimony.

STATEMENT OF JOSEPH F. MARTIN, ACTING DIRECTOR, HOMELAND SECURITY ENTERPRISE AND FIRST RESPONDERS GROUP, SCIENCE AND TECHNOLOGY DIRECTORATE, U.S. DEPARTMENT OF HOMELAND SECURITY

Mr. MARTIN. Good afternoon, Chairman Ratcliffe, Ranking Member Richmond, and Ranking Member Thompson, and distinguished Members of the subcommittee. Thank you for inviting me here this afternoon.

My name is Jay Martin. I am the acting director of S&T's First Responders Group. As a first responder for over 20 years here in the National capital region, I understand the needs of the first-responder community and the potential that innovative technology can have on issues of emerging threats.

DHS and our Nation's first responders operate in an evolving environment of both threats and opportunities. Our accelerating pace of risk and technology development loom over every mission in the Department. S&T's approach to R&D allows us to be more agile in helping our partners stay ahead of the threats and seize available opportunities.

Recognizing the needs of our partners, S&T leans forward in engaging the end-user community to bring more focus to our work. We leverage technical expertise in critical areas that touch on all aspects of operations. We partner with emerging innovation leaders in industry, like wearable-technology developers. We strive to bring new solutions to widespread operational use in the homeland security enterprise.

As part of being more forward-leaning, S&T recently finalized five visionary goals—cross-cutting goals that focus our work around common objectives. These align with Congressional direction, support Departmental policy, and address strategic challenges and threats identified by the homeland security enterprise.

Our goals include: Screening at speed—that is, security that matches the pace of life; a trusted cyber future—protecting privacy, commerce, and community; enable the decision maker—actionable information at the speed of thought; responder of the future—protected, connected, and fully aware; and, finally, resilient communities—disaster-proofing society.

To achieve these visionary goals, S&T built a prioritized portfolio around Apex programs. Apex is focused on the most challenging homeland security problems to take a broad approach to reaching these goals, not a single-technology solution.

Since S&T's first Apex began with the Secret Service in 2010, we have helped partners identify efficiencies, save money, and integrate emerging technologies. For example, my group leads the Next Generation First Responder Apex. This program will enable first responders to make faster decisions, be more efficient, and operate safer as they respond to threats and disasters.

Our Apex program is focused on unique challenges faced by fully-networked responders and is considering the cybersecurity impacts in all aspects of emerging technologies. This includes wearable technologies, advanced communications, and enhanced personal protective equipment.

Across this Nation, over 70,000 Federal, State, local, Tribal, and territorial agencies are responsible for public safety and emergency response. S&T's ability to build partnerships is critical to supporting their efforts. S&T tailors its business model to succeed with these responders, including DHS operational components like my colleagues on the panel.

Industry engagement is fundamental, and our programs are innovative, not only in outreach to responder and commercial entities but also in the use of alternative approaches to conduct research and development. Price competitions and a consolidation and integration of international markets are examples of ways that we are evolving how S&T does business.

One of S&T's highest priority areas is in reinforcing response and recovery to a potential radiological or nuclear event. We work in conjunction with DNDO on pre-incident operations and with FEMA, Department of Energy, and EPA on response and recovery. S&T focuses lab and academia experts on the immediate problem of how to prepare and use equipment already in the hands of first responders if a radiological nuclear event were to occur. Our work enables State and local responders to increase their capabilities and to respond in the first minutes, hours, and days of an emergency.

S&T conducts research development, testing, and evaluation to secure our Nation's critical information infrastructure and to plan for a more secure cyber future. S&T works to create partnerships between Government and private industry, the venture-capital community and the research community, including academia and National laboratories.

Among our priorities is the financial sector, who we work with to ensure market reliability and cyber protection, as well as with the first responders on identity credentials and access management. S&T also assists in transforming cybersecurity technologies from research labs to the homeland security enterprise and the commercial marketplace.

As our work with first responders demonstrates, we use technology as a force multiplier to enhance responder capabilities. We are also working with industry in new ways to use evolving technology to its fullest by integrating it into our approaches.

Thank you for inviting me to appear before you today. I appreciate the opportunity to testify, and I will be pleased to answer your questions.

[The prepared statement of Mr. Martin follows:]

PREPARED STATEMENT OF JOSEPH F. MARTIN

FEBRUARY 12, 2014

Good morning Chairman Ratcliffe, Ranking Member Richmond, and distinguished Members of the subcommittee. Thank you for the opportunity to testify before you today on the role of the Department of Homeland Security's (DHS) Science and Technology Directorate (S&T). S&T's mission is to help strengthen America's security and resiliency by providing assessments, analysis, and reports and developing innovative technology solutions for the Homeland Security Enterprise. In this testimony, I will discuss how technology shapes today's threat environment, empowering homeland security operators and first responders with new capabilities but also enabling malevolent actors. To address this, S&T helps operators harness and utilize technology, scientific knowledge, and engineering as a force multiplier and, where possible, to gain leap-ahead capabilities. To illustrate the role of technology and how S&T delivers it to the Homeland Security Enterprise, I will talk about S&T's experience with first responders and how we work with them to overcome gaps and achieve their missions more effectively, efficiently, and safely.

Today, S&T and the Homeland Security Enterprise exist in an environment of rapidly-evolving threats and opportunities, and the accelerating pace of risk and technological development loom over every mission in the Department. Threats now range from lone-wolf violent extremists to non-state actors with state-like capabilities to rogue states with increasingly sophisticated abilities. In the past, only state actors had the resources and technical capacity necessary to create extreme levels of destruction and disruption. Today, individual actors have access to technology that is sufficient to make explosive devices, develop biological weapons, or execute sophisticated cyber attacks. The wide variation of potential malicious actors—ranging from individuals to terrorist groups to state actors—each have a wide range of capabilities and options to carry out acts that pose immense challenges to homeland security operators. All of this is compounded by the accelerating evolution and revolution of technology. The fields of manufacturing and material sciences, information technology, and biosciences have made revolutionary gains in the last decade. With the commercial sector, particularly small and medium-sized business, driving innovation and with trends like the maker movement proliferating and democratizing technology, new homeland security challenges and opportunities continue to mount.

REINVENTING R&D TO BE MORE MODERN AND AGILE

The traditional Federal model for research and development (R&D) is based on decades-old assumptions that, in many cases, are ill-suited to today's environment and can stifle innovation in Government. Federal funding still drives the majority of basic and applied research, but private-sector investment focused on late-stage development surpassed Government's total annual R&D investments in the 1980s and has continued this trend. In homeland security, innovation cycles in areas like advanced analytics, communications, additive manufacturing, and cyber occur so quickly that traditional Government vehicles for investment and acquisition struggle to keep up with advances and changes in technology.

Recognizing the growing need for homeland security-tailored technology paired with an evolving innovation ecosystem that includes greater investment by the private sector, S&T is reinventing its approach to R&D to be more agile in helping our partners stay ahead of threat trends. We are becoming more forward-leaning, bringing more focus to our portfolio, and engaging more effectively with industry. We are dedicating a portion of our R&D programs to leveraging technical expertise in critical areas that touch on all aspects of operation (e.g., data analytics, network security). We are partnering with emerging innovation leaders in industry and shifting our R&D and testing and evaluation toward DHS component-based innovation centers focused on bringing new solutions to wide-spread operational use. Taken together, this will make S&T a more capable R&D agent for homeland security operators and first responders.

S&T's Visionary Goals

As part of being more forward-leaning, S&T recently finalized five visionary goals as North Star-like objectives. To arrive at the five goals below, S&T used an inclusive, transparent platform to garner input not only from all of S&T but also from our partners and stakeholders inside and outside of Government. The goals are cross-cutting and coalesce S&T around common objectives, align with Departmental doctrine and policy, and address strategic challenges and threats identified by the Homeland Security Enterprise. Finally, and perhaps most importantly, the Visionary Goals inspire and excite the science and technology ecosystem around ambitious, innovative solutions.

- *Screening At Speed: Security that Matches the Pace of Life.*—Noninvasive screening at speed will provide for comprehensive protection while adapting security to the pace of life rather than life to security. With safeguards to protect privacy, unobtrusive screening of people, baggage, or cargo will enable the seamless detection of threats with minimal impact on the pace of travel and speed of commerce.
- *A Trusted Cyber Future: Protecting Privacy, Commerce, and Community.*—In a future of increasing cyber connections, underlying digital infrastructure will be self-detecting, self-protecting, and self-healing. Users will trust that information is protected, illegal use is deterred, and privacy is not compromised. Security will operate seamlessly in the background.
- *Enable the Decision Maker: Actionable Information at the Speed of Thought.*— Predictive analytics, risk analysis, and modeling and simulation systems will enable critical and proactive decisions to be made based on the most relevant information, transforming data into actionable information. Even in the face of uncertain environments involving chemical, biological, radiological, or nuclear incidents, accurate, credible, and context-based information will empower the decision maker to take instant actions to improve critical outcomes.
- *Responder of the Future: Protected, Connected, and Fully Aware.*—The responder of the future is threat-adaptive and cross-functional. Armed with comprehensive physical protection, interoperable tools, and networked threat detection and mitigation capabilities, responders of the future will be better able to serve their communities.
- *Resilient Communities: Disaster-Resilience for the Future.*—Critical infrastructure of the future will be designed, built, and maintained to be resilient to naturally-occurring and man-made disasters. Decision makers will know when a disaster is coming, anticipate the effects, and use already-in-place or rapidly deployed countermeasures to shield communities from negative consequences. Resilient communities struck by disasters will not only bounce back but bounce back quicker.

In establishing S&T's Visionary Goals, we took a major step forward in creating two-way dialogue around our work. This crowdsourcing shaped our final product with additional feedback that we would not necessarily have otherwise been able to tap into. As a natural extension, we created the National Conversation on Homeland Security Technology, which brings together all interested parties (responders, operational users, citizens, academia, and industry to name a few) to play a role in shaping the future of homeland security technology. Through on-line forums and in-person discussions, we will foster understanding of the homeland security market and build progress toward outcomes that will keep us all safer and minimize disruption to the pace of daily life.

USING SCIENCE AND TECHNOLOGY TO ADDRESS FIRST RESPONDER OPERATIONAL NEEDS

To look at the role of technology and how S&T delivers new capabilities to the Homeland Security Enterprise, an illustrative example is our work for the responder community. More than 70,000 Federal, State, local, Tribal, and territorial and entities support public safety and emergency response in every community across the Nation. First responders cross disciplines, including law enforcement, fire services, emergency medical services and emergency management, and serve communities of widely-ranging sizes and specific needs against a backdrop of complex operational realities and limitations.

First responders also face a myriad of threats that materialize in various fire, natural disaster, terrorism, and mass casualty emergencies. As a result, responder organizations must plan for wide-ranging response including routine, day-to-day duties as well as rare, catastrophic events. Those organizations also face the challenge of furnishing responders with equipment and training that enable all-hazard response to rare events without interfering with routine duties.

To identify common gaps and address the most pressing responder needs, S&T has an organization within the Directorate—its First Responders Group (FRG)—dedicated to strengthening first responder safety and effectiveness. S&T, through FRG, focuses on evolving, high-impact threats and how to prepare responders without disrupting day-to-day operational duties. Example projects include all-hazard communications and data interoperability, situational awareness, and personal protective equipment as well as more specific work in radiological/nuclear response and recovery. As new threats emerge, S&T works with the first responder community to identify and fill resulting capability gaps guided by several principles for identifying solutions:

- *Operational Needs Drive Projects.*—Recognizing that initiatives must be based on user needs and driven from responders in the field.
- *Building on Existing Investments.*—Encouraging efficiencies by building on existing investments saves money by avoiding unnecessary and duplicative development of new hardware, software, data development, and training.
- *Leveraging Existing Solutions.*—Conducting technology foraging to help leverage existing interagency and private-sector solutions before any investments in new solutions are made.
- *Forming Partnerships.*—Building partnerships across Federal, State, local, Tribal, and territorial agencies as well as with international partners to maximize funding and increase adoption.
- *Daily Use Solutions.*—Seeking technological solutions that improve not only catastrophic response but daily use by first responders.
- *Non-Proprietary Solutions.*—Ensuring that technologies from different manufacturers can actually interoperate requires the use of open-source, non-proprietary solutions and standards-based approaches.
- *Affordable and Accessible Solutions.*—Recognizing that solutions need to be affordable and commercially available for purchase.

As you will see detailed below, S&T tailors its business model to succeed with State, local, Tribal, and territorial first responders in addition to DHS operational components including the Domestic Nuclear Detection Office (DNDO), National Protection and Programs Directorate (NPPD), and Secret Service. Industry engagement is fundamental, and our programs are innovative not only in outreach to responder and commercial communities but also in use of funding vehicles. Prize competitions and consolidation and integration of international markets, for example, draw down risk to industry and incentivize product development.

First responder engagement at every stage of development

FRG engages end-users at every stage of the technology development process. By engaging end-users at the beginning of the technology development cycle for requirements and then continuing throughout the R&D process, FRG fosters user-produced innovation and ensures that the solutions developed have a high probability of being transitioned to the field. Prototypes will then be commercialized, deployed, and adopted as rapidly as possible. For fielded technologies, this enhances wide-spread adoption of these technologies in the field. This early and frequent engagement also helps FRG to better align current and future investments with responders' highest-priority needs.

First responder capability gaps are identified through a series of studies that culminate in a knowledge product known as Project Responder, which describes the highest-priority needs for catastrophic incident response. The latest iteration, Project Responder 4, focuses on identifying high priority capability needs, shortfalls, and priorities for catastrophic incident response. It identifies a set of enduring and emerging capability needs, frames them into technology objectives, and assesses the state of science and technology to meet those needs. Findings are based on discussions with Federal, State, and local first responders as well as technical subject-matter experts. These interactions ensure that potential solutions reflect operational considerations and are based on an actionable and achievable technology path or roadmap. With Project Responder as a foundation, FRG uses its First Responder Resource Group, consisting of more than 120 first responders and representatives of National first responder associations, to translate broad capability gaps and needs into defined, validated requirements, performance measures, and concepts of operations that can be incorporated into FRG's solicitations for projects. Recent requirements have ranged from location information and proximity to risk for responders to communication in any environmental condition to versatile clothing and equipment that protects against multiple hazards.

After identifying requirements, FRG conducts internal and external technology foraging to determine who else is working in this space and what partial or complete solutions may already exist. Wherever possible, existing investments by Federal partners, academia, and the private sector are leveraged. FRG selects projects for funding based on a number of criteria including the practitioner-identified gaps, criticality/operational impact, threat likelihood, applicability, state of the science, cost-benefit analysis, ease of integration, transition likelihood, and time needed to prototype. Responders work with FRG program managers throughout the life cycle of each project and assist DHS in creating awareness in the field of these newly-developed solutions.

Ultimately, S&T teams with the first responder community and commercial sector to transition technologies, standards, and knowledge products and integrate them into regular use. As solutions develop into mature, commercial products, they ultimately can be purchased by first responder organizations through the Federal Emergency Management Agency's (FEMA) Authorized Equipment List (AEL), which is a list of equipment approved for purchase using FEMA grants. As a service to first responders, FRG also provides objective buying advice for first responders looking at the AEL to help them make informed purchase decisions. The System Assessment and Validation for Emergency Responders (SAVER) program conducts objective assessments and validations of commercial off-the-shelf equipment and publishes explanations for different tools and technologies and their application. After S&T has helped commercialize a product and published it on the AEL, we still work with responders through FirstResponder.gov and other Federal R&D agencies such as the National Institute of Justice to promote awareness and enable informed procurement decisions in the first responder community.

Radiological/nuclear response and recovery

One of FRG's highest-priority areas is reinforcing response and recovery to a potential radiological or nuclear event. The detonation of a radiological dispersal device or improvised nuclear device (IND) has the potential to cause significant casualties, economic disruption, and critical infrastructure destruction. Responding to and recovering from such an event poses unique challenges to responder organizations. S&T, through its National Urban Security Technology Laboratory (NUSTL), works in conjunction with DNDO on pre-incident operations and with FEMA, the Department of Energy (DOE), and the Environmental Protection Agency (EPA) on response and recovery. A distinguishing aspect of S&T's program is that, recognizing the significant lag between development of new technology and broad deployment with responders, S&T focuses lab and academia experts on the immediate problem of how to prepare and use equipment already in the hands of first responders if a radiological or nuclear event were to occur. S&T's products and science-based guidance (e.g., how to manage complex incident data, methods to mitigate community exposure to radiation hazards) go directly to State and local responders, increasing their capabilities to respond in the first minutes, hours, and days of a radiological emergency.

The foundation for S&T's work was analysis of significant but broadly dispersed work already completed or under way in the field combined with direct interaction with local agencies to understand their major roadblocks in preparing for radiological response. This was documented and synthesized in the *DHS S&T Radio-*

logical/Nuclear Response and Recovery Research and Development Investment Plan.
Based on the plan, the related portfolio now consists of 10 individual activities serving a broad coalition of stakeholders. Examples include the following:

- Compiling guidance and best practices on radiological particle containment, rapid gross-decontamination, and early phase waste management into an electronic application, making it easy for local agency decision makers and responders in the field to access key information.
- Revisiting scientific research and publications related to radiological dispersal device response to make guidance actionable for first responders through tools and preparedness efforts.
- Improving radiological data management and modeling technology used by specialized Federal agencies and making it more easily available and accessible to State and local agencies to increase operational capability and also increase communication and coordination between levels of government.

Another S&T project of interest is the Radiological Emergency Management System (REMS), which is a network of gamma radiation detectors that provides emergency managers with information on environmental radiation levels to support response and recovery operations in the event of a radiological or nuclear event. REMS was designed at NUSTL in coordination with DNDO and commercialized by a major instrument manufacturer. The New York Police Department, which has a deep relationship with NUSTL, has purchased and deployed dozens of REMS sensors as part of its operational system and stands as a baseline for potential use in other major metropolitan areas.

Though S&T's investment in radiological/nuclear response and recovery is relatively young, the portfolio is making a significant impact by leveraging millions of dollars in previous and on-going investments by DNDO, FEMA, the Department of Defense, EPA, and DOE and by taking advantage of long-standing relationships with DHS components like DNDO and FEMA with operational missions in this space.

Next Generation First Responder Apex program

Since S&T's first Apex program began with the Secret Service in 2010, Apex programs have been some of our most successful. With recent expansion of Apexes as a portion of S&T's portfolio, much of the original Apex structure will remain—these will still be cross-cutting, multi-disciplinary efforts intended to solve problems of strategic operational importance—but the projects are being scaled to apply to a wider portion of the portfolio and will operate on longer 5-year time lines. The Next Generation First Responder (NGFR) Apex program vision is first responders who are protected, connected, and fully aware and capable of faster, more efficient, and safer response to threats and disasters of all types. NGFR is developing an integrated and modular ensemble that includes an enhanced duty uniform, personal protective equipment (PPE), wearable computing and sensing technology, and robust communication capability. The modularity and flexibility of NGFR's approach promotes affordability while still supporting diverse environments, including PPE and duty uniforms enhanced for fire resistance, liquid resistance and splash protection, puncture resistance, and improved usability and comfort.

NGFR is harnessing the best existing and emerging technologies and integrating them into a well-defined and standards-based open architecture. A fundamental element of NGFR's strategy to accomplish this will be tapping into the dynamic and growing market for wearable sensors and smart technology. It will use innovative outreach and funding vehicles like prize competitions to bring in innovative corners of the market that have not historically partnered with the Federal Government. NGFR will ultimately be able to provide real-time situation awareness and give previously unattainable recognition and avoidance of hazards before, during, and after incidents.

To support NGFR and many other projects, S&T is also being more innovative in its interface with the international first responder community. First responders around the globe share a common mission to ensure the safety and security of the people they serve. They are often asked to respond to complex incidents like the Deep Water Horizon oil spill and Fukushima Daiichi nuclear disaster. Most countries collaborate at an international level but largely address responder challenges independently and face funding challenges, duplicate effort, and struggle to gain traction in a fragmented global market. To facilitate more robust cooperation and build a larger market for global first responder needs, S&T leads the International Forum to Advance First Responder Technology. The forum is a government-sponsored platform for the following:

- Defining a common set of capability gaps across the globe;
- Using assessments of global markets and opportunities to inform prioritization;

- Providing a platform for international collaboration on R&D initiatives and solutions;
- Engaging industry throughout, to prepare it to make advanced technology available at affordable prices.

The forum initially consists of government representatives from S&T's 13 bilateral partners, Finland, and Japan. It will give responders a global voice and use common problem sets and standards to create or broaden global markets for first responder technology. Ultimately, this lowers risk for industry and incentivizes investment in more robust capabilities and product lines.

Identity, Credential, and Access Management

To protect first responder voice and data communications, assuring secure access to networks and systems is critical. This requires the registration, verification, authentication, and authorization of network users. This technology area is commonly called Identity, Credential, and Access Management (ICAM). FRG, in close partnership with S&T's Cyber Security Division, NPPD's Office of Emergency Communication (OEC), the DHS Office of the Chief Information Officer, the White House's Program Manager for the Information Sharing Environment (PM–ISE), and other partners, is developing ICAM approaches for the Nation's public safety community. While many ICAM solutions do exist today, significant interoperability issues remain for many technical and policy reasons. This leads most public safety officials to maintain multiple cyber identities to perform their job, which is not only inefficient but also adds security risks.

With more than 60 percent of the public safety community leveraging communication and information-sharing capabilities of broadband services, S&T has a responsibility to help secure communications and data across these networks. This is an increasingly complex problem, but we collaborate with our partners to address this by developing and proliferating standards-based approaches that align with Federal ICAM guidance. Related to this problem, S&T must assure that ICAM practices of the future (NPSBN) will meet the security needs of the public safety community and be interoperable with the practices of other networks. FirstNet is an independent authority charged with implementing a single wireless broadband data-sharing network, the NPSBN, primarily for public safety personnel. Ultimately, more than 5 million members of the public safety community may use FirstNet, and S&T, along with other public and private partners will help ensure the security and dependability of communications across the NPSBN for first responders.

In January 2015, with our partners, the PM–ISE, and the International Association of Chiefs of Police, S&T released a report recommending principles and actions for developing an ICAM interoperability strategy that will focus on registering, verifying, and authorizing network users. While this strategy focuses on FirstNet, the principles and actions will be relevant to any initiative that needs to identify and authorize users for access to secure resources. We will continue to work with our partners, in particular PM–ISE and NPPD OEC, to address immediate and longer-term needs of first responders on high-priority ICAM issues.

CONCLUSION

Today, I discussed how technology shapes today's threat environment as a double-edged sword, empowering operators and first responders on one hand but enabling malevolent actors and raising the risk of complex technological disasters on the other. As our work with first responders demonstrates, S&T is helping the Homeland Security Enterprise harness and utilize technology as a force multiplier and to gain leap-ahead capabilities.

Thank you for inviting me to appear before you today. I appreciate the opportunity to testify and would be pleased to answer any questions you may have.

Mr. RATCLIFFE. Thanks very much, Mr. Martin.

The Chairman would now like to recognize Mr. Noonan to testify.

STATEMENT OF WILLIAM NOONAN, DEPUTY SPECIAL AGENT IN CHARGE, CRIMINAL INVESTIGATIVE DIVISION, U.S. SECRET SERVICE

Mr. NOONAN. Good afternoon, Chairman Ratcliffe, Ranking Member Richmond, Ranking Member Thompson, and distinguished Members of the subcommittee. Thank you for the opportunity to testify with our DHS partners regarding the evolving threat of cyber crime to our Nation and our work to research and develop technologies that aid us in countering new and emerging threats.

The Secret Service continues our founding mission to investigate crimes impacting our Nation's financial system. Over the past several decades, our financial system has increasingly become dependent on information technology. As a result, criminals motivated by greed have adapted their methods and are using cyber space to steal sensitive information for use in highly profitable fraud schemes and other illicit activities.

The wealth accrued by the world's most skilled cyber criminals is staggering. Most have become multi-millionaires through their criminal endeavors, and they are not stopping there.

Current cybersecurity efforts are being outpaced by criminals, who reinvest their illicit proceeds to strengthen their cyber capabilities. Over the past 10 years, the Secret Service has observed the development of transnational cyber criminals into highly-capable adversaries. They routinely compromise highly secure computer networks, they accomplish increasingly profitable schemes, they enable the malicious cyber operations of others, and they undermine the rule of law in order to protect their criminal enterprises.

Rich off the money they have stolen from Americans, our Nation faces increasing risk that sophisticated cyber criminals may coordinate their unique skill sets and combined expertise to conduct cyber attacks against our critical infrastructure.

In considering all the high-profile cyber incidents this past year, it is clear that defense alone is inadequate. Proactive law enforcement investigations are essential in combating these threats. Conducting these investigations is what drives our work at the Secret Service. We focus on investigating the most capable cyber criminals, those individuals and groups that continue to reinvest their profits in growing capability.

To combat these criminals, the Secret Service works closely with our partners at DHS's Science and Technology and National Protection and Programs Directorates in addition to our partners in academia and the private sector to research and develop technologies to enhance our operations.

Through our international network of Electronic Crimes Task Forces, the Secret Service partners with over 4,000 private-sector organizations; 2,500 international, Federal, State, and local law enforcement agencies; and over 350 academic partners.

Just to highlight three examples of where Secret Service works with our academic partners: At Carnegie Mellon University, the Secret Service has assigned special agents to the CERT Coordination Center since 1998. Through this partnership, the Secret Service has been able to develop and field innovative technologies that enable the Secret Service to both investigate and protect against cyber threats. It is through this partnership at Carnegie Mellon that the Secret Service first established the Critical Systems Protection Program in 2001 and continues to develop and field technologies to secure the critical systems that our protective mission depends on.

At the University of Tulsa, the Secret Service established the Cell Phone Forensic Facility in 2008 to understand threats involving mobile devices and support law enforcement investigations.

This facility continues to be a global center of excellence in those fields, continually developing new methods for recovering evidence from mobile devices and performing the most challenging of forensic exams—those involving damaged devices. This facility is an excellent example of an effective academic partnership, where students conduct work and research that directly address some of the most challenging problems we face.

At the University of Texas, Austin, the Secret Service is a member of the Center for Identity and serves on its board of advisors. The Center for Identity was established in 2010 and is focused on researching the identity ecosystem and strengthening our ability to counter identity theft and other emerging identity-related threats.

The work of our private and academic partners is critical for the Secret Service to keep pace with the changing use of technologies by adversaries who target our homeland.

As this panel demonstrates, cyber crime is just one of several challenges at the intersection of technology and security that our Department is charged with countering. We at the Secret Service are committed to continuing to adapt and innovate the performance of our integrated mission.

Thank you for the opportunity to testify, and I look forward to your questions.

[The prepared statement of Mr. Noonan follows:]

PREPARED STATEMENT OF WILLIAM NOONAN

FEBRUARY 12, 2015

Good morning Chairman Ratcliffe, Ranking Member Richmond, and distinguished Members of the subcommittee. Thank you for the opportunity to testify on the Secret Service's progressive efforts to protect our homeland by countering cyber criminal activity.

The cyber crime threats to our homeland continue to rapidly grow fuelled by the wealth these illicit activities are generating. For over three decades the Secret Service has investigated cyber criminal activity[1] and worked to counter some of the most proficient transnational cyber criminal groups. Based on our experience investigating and apprehending many of the most capable and prolific transnational cyber criminals, I hope to provide this committee with useful insight into the continued threat our Nation faces from malicious cyber activity.

THE TRANSNATIONAL CYBER CRIME THREAT

Nearly 15 years ago, advances in computer technology and greater access to personally identifiable information (PII) via the internet created on-line marketplaces for transnational cyber criminals to share stolen information and criminal methodologies. This has resulted in a steady increase in the quality, quantity, and complexity of cyber crimes targeting private industry and critical infrastructure. These crimes include network intrusions, hacking attacks, and account takeovers leading to significant data breaches affecting every sector of the economy. Recently reported payment card data breaches are examples of this long-term trend of major data breaches perpetrated by transnational cyber criminals who are intent on targeting our Nation's financial payment system for illicit gain.

The wealth accrued by the world's most capable cyber criminals is staggering. Some have become millionaires through their cyber criminal activities, even buying numerous resort properties in tropical locations. More significantly they are reinvesting what they have stolen to develop increasingly sophisticated cyber capabilities and organizations to perpetuate and expand their illicit schemes. The capabilities these criminals develop are increasingly being used by foreign states for intelligence collection or military purposes.

---

[1] Congress established 18 USC § 1029–1030 as part of the Comprehensive Crime Control Act of 1984 and explicitly assigned the Secret Service authority to investigate these criminal violations.

The collaboration amongst top tier cyber-criminals is astounding. These individuals routinely trust one another with millions of dollars as they execute their highly distributed transnational criminal conspiracies. These groups have increasingly segmented their operations, allowing for the development of highly-talented specialists in performing each part of the criminal schemes: From gaining unauthorized access to protected computer networks, to engaging in sophisticated frauds, to laundering and distributing their proceeds. These growing specialties raise both the complexity of investigating these cases, as well as the level of potential harm to companies and individuals.

For example, illicit underground cyber crime marketplaces allow criminals to buy, sell, and trade malicious software, access to sensitive networks, spamming services, payment card data, PII, bank account information, brokerage account information, hacking services, and counterfeit identity documents. These illicit digital marketplaces vary in size, with some of the more popular sites boasting membership of approximately 80,000 users and some sites being highly exclusive invitation-only associations. These digital marketplaces often use various digital currencies, and cyber criminals have made extensive use of digital currencies to pay for criminal goods and services or launder illicit proceeds.

THE SECRET SERVICE STRATEGY FOR COMBATING THIS THREAT

The Secret Service proactively investigates cyber crime using a variety of investigative means to often infiltrate these transnational cyber criminal groups and counter every element of their criminal schemes. As a result of these proactive investigations, the Secret Service is often the first to learn of planned or on-going data breaches and is quick to notify affected companies and institutions with actionable information to mitigate the damage from the data breach and terminate the criminal's unauthorized access to their networks. Victim companies rarely identify unauthorized access to their networks; rather law enforcement, financial institutions, or other third parties identify and notify the likely victim company of a data breach.

A trusted relationship with the victim is essential for confirming the crime, remediating the situation, beginning a criminal investigation, and collecting evidence. To foster these trusted relationships, in 2001, Congress directed the Secret Service to develop a National network of electronic crimes task forces, based on our existing New York Electronic Crimes Task Force, for the purpose of preventing, detecting, and investigating various forms of electronic crimes, including potential terrorist cyber attacks against critical infrastructure and financial payment systems. Today the Secret Service operates a global network of 38 Electronic Crimes Task Forces (ECTF) as part of this growing network. These ECTFs are the foundation for the Secret Service's investigations of cyber crime and our primary means of sharing actionable information with potential victim companies. For example, in 2014, based on information discovered through just one of our on-going cyber crime investigations, the Secret Service notified hundreds of U.S. entities of cyber criminal activity targeting their organizations.

The Secret Service also invests in developing the capabilities of our State and local partners. In partnership with the State of Alabama, the Secret Service operates the National Computer Forensic Institute (NCFI) to train State and local law enforcement investigators, prosecutors, and judges in how to conduct computer forensic examinations, respond to network intrusion incidents, and conduct cyber crimes investigations. Graduates of NCFI typically join the Secret Service's network of ECTFs, and have frequently made vital contributions to significant Secret Service investigations of transnational cyber criminals.

As the Secret Service investigates cyber crime, we discover new and emerging cyber criminal methods and share relevant cybersecurity information broadly to enable other organizations to secure their networks while protecting on-going investigations and the privacy and civil rights of all involved. The Secret Service accomplishes these objectives through contributions to industry-leading annual reports like the Verizon Data Breach Investigations Report and the Trustwave Global Security Report, and through more immediate reports, including joint Malware Initial Findings Reports (MIFRs).

For example, this year UPS Stores Inc. used information published in a joint report on the Back-Off malware to protect itself and its customers from cyber criminal activity.[2] The information in this report was derived from a Secret Service investigation of a network intrusion at a small retailer in Syracuse, New York. The Secret Service partnered with the National Cybersecurity & Communications Integration Center (NCCIC/US–CERT) and the Financial Services Information Sharing and

---

[2] See *http://www.us-cert.gov/security-publications/Backoff-Point-Sale-Malware.*

Analysis Center (FS–ISAC) to widely share actionable cybersecurity information derived from this investigation to help numerous other organizations, while protecting the integrity of the on-going investigation and the privacy of all parties. For UPS Stores, Inc., the result was the identification of 51 stores in 24 States that had been impacted, enabling UPS Stores, Inc. to contain and mitigate this cyber incident before it developed into a major data breach.[3]

As we share cybersecurity information discovered in the course of our criminal investigations, we also continue pursuing our investigation in order to apprehend and bring to justice those involved. Due to the inherent challenges in investigating transnational crime, particularly the lack of cooperation of some countries with U.S. law enforcement investigations, occasionally it can take years to finally apprehend the top tier criminals. The Secret Service works closely with its partners in the Departments of Justice and State to develop the capabilities of foreign law enforcement partners and to foster collaboration.

For example, in July of 2014 Secret Service agents arrested Roman Seleznev of Vladivostok, Russia, through an international law enforcement operation. Mr. Seleznev has been charged in Seattle in a 40-count indictment for allegedly being involved in the theft and sale of financial information of millions of customers. Seleznev is also charged in a separate indictment with participating in a racketeer influenced corrupt organization (RICO) and conspiracy related to possession of counterfeit and unauthorized access devices.[4] This investigation was led by the Secret Service's Seattle Electronic Crimes Task Force.

In another case, the Secret Service, as part of a joint investigation with U.S. Immigration and Customs Enforcement's Homeland Security Investigations (HSI) and the Global Illicit Financial Team (GIFT), hosted by IRS-Criminal Investigations, shut down the digital currency provider Liberty Reserve, which was allegedly widely used by criminals worldwide to store, transfer, and launder the proceeds of a variety of illicit activities. In addition, the Treasury Department's Financial Crimes Enforcement Network found Liberty Reserve to be a financial institution of primary money laundering concern pursuant to Section 311 of the USA PATRIOT Act. Liberty Reserve had more than 1 million users, who conducted approximately 55 million transactions through its system totaling more than $6 billion in funds. The founder of Liberty Reserve, Arthur Budovsky, was recently extradited from Spain to the United States. Mr. Budovsky is among seven individuals charged in the indictment. Four co-defendants—Vladimir Kats, Azzeddine el Amine, Mark Marmilev, and Maxim Chukharev—have pleaded guilty and await sentencing. Charges against Liberty Reserve and two individual defendants, who have not been apprehended, remain pending. This investigation was led by the Secret Service's New York Electronic Crimes Task Force.

LEGISLATIVE ACTION TO COMBAT DATA BREACHES

While there is no technology available to prevent data breaches of U.S. customer information, legislative action could help to improve the Nation's cybersecurity, reduce regulatory costs on U.S. companies, and strengthen law enforcement's ability to conduct effective investigations. In January, the administration proposed law enforcement provisions related to computer security, highlighting the importance of additional tools to combat emerging criminal practices.[5] We continue to support changes like these that will assist us in countering the rapidly-evolving threat of cyber crime.

CONCLUSION

The Secret Service is committed to continuing to safeguard the Nation's financial payment systems by defeating cyber criminal organizations. Responding to the growth of these types of crimes, and the level of sophistication these criminals employ, requires significant resources and substantial collaboration among law enforcement and its public and private-sector partners. Accordingly, the Secret Service dedicates significant resources to improving investigative techniques, providing training for law enforcement partners, and sharing information on cyber threats. The Secret Service will continue to coordinate and collaborate with other Government agencies and the private sector as we develop new methods for combating cyber crime. Thank you for your continued commitment to protecting our Nation's financial system from cyber crime.

---

[3] See UPS Store's press release. Available at: *http://www.theupsstore.com/about/media-room/Pages/The-ups-storenotifies-customers.aspx*.

[4] See *http://www.justice.gov/usao/waw/press/2014/October/seleznev.html*.

[5] This proposal is available at: *http://www.whitehouse.gov/omb/legislative_letters/*.

Mr. RATCLIFFE. Thanks very much, Mr. Noonan.

Last but not least, the Chairman would like to recognize Mr. Painter to testify.

STATEMENT OF WILLIAM PAINTER, ANALYST, GOVERNMENT AND FINANCE DIVISION, CONGRESSIONAL RESEARCH SERVICE, LIBRARY OF CONGRESS

Mr. PAINTER. Good afternoon, Chairman Ratcliffe, Ranking Member Richmond, Ranking Member Thompson, and distinguished Members of the subcommittee. Thank you for inviting me to appear before you today to discuss how DHS's budget situation could affect the Department's efforts to develop new technologies and confront emerging threats.

I will discuss three potential scenarios for the fiscal year 2015 DHS appropriations and examine what each could entail for the Department going forward. As you know, Congress has not, to date, provided annual appropriations for DHS but, instead, provided an extension of funding for the Department through a continuing resolution, or CR, that expires on February 27.

At least three possible immediate futures for DHS appropriations exist. First is extension of the CR. The second is enactment of a fiscal year 2015 annual appropriations bill or, third, a lapse in annual discretionary appropriations.

First, extension. So far, in fiscal year 2015, DHS has been operating under a series of interim CRs, which typically provide temporary funding at a given rate of operations rather than a set level for the year. Interim CRs expire at a specified date prior to the end of the fiscal year. A second type of CR is the full-year CR, which provides funding all the way through to the end of the fiscal year. DHS has operated under the terms of such a CR only once, in fiscal year 2011.

To preserve Congressional prerogatives, Congress generally places several restrictions on the use of funding provided under an interim CR. These include a prohibition on the start of new projects, prohibiting funding decisions, including grants, that would impinge on Congress' final funding prerogatives, and allowing only the most limited funding action permitted in the resolution to continue the Government's work.

As a result of these restrictions and uncertainty over when they may be lifted and annual funding levels finally set, an agency funded under an interim CR experiences several challenges.

A CR may provide funding at a higher or lower rate than needed to carry out Departmental priorities. For example, under the current CR, S&T is being allocated funds as a rate higher than needed for construction of the National Bio and Agro-Defense Facility, while DNDO is getting funds at a much lower rate than it needs to buy radiation detectors for front-line DHS personnel. This mismatch is not on the basis of an affirmative policy decision by Congress. It is simply because those programs need to change from the previous year's baseline, and the funding stream did not.

Timing can also be an issue. After an interim CR is replaced, a Department may not have time to use some of the funding it has been provided before it expires at the end of the fiscal year. Although most of the budget for DNDO and S&T can be used up to

3 to 5 years after it was appropriated, most of NPPD's appropriation expires at the end of each fiscal year.

The second potential scenario is enactment of an annual appropriations bill. This would allow DHS to carry out its mission with transparent and explicit direction from Congress in terms of funding levels for its many missions. DHS would be able to hire staff, initiate new projects, and award grants within the parameters laid out in the enacted legislation and accompanying explanatory statement.

The third possible scenario is what would occur in the event that the current CR expires without extension or replacement. Annual appropriations for DHS would lapse. DHS would be required to implement a shutdown furlough, as they did in the Government-wide lapse in appropriations in October 2013. This would represent a disruption in DHS operations and raise obstacles to efficient management and oversight much greater than those raised by an interim continuing resolution. In 2013, roughly 85 percent of the Department's functions continued during the shutdown, but 96 percent of S&T, 95 percent of DNDO, and 43 percent of NPPD staff were furloughed.

DHS personnel who are legally permitted to continue to work in the event of a lapse generally fall into two categories: Those with activities that are not funded through 1-year appropriations and those whose work is exempted under specific authorities of the Antideficiency Act. Among the components of interest today, only the Office of Biometric Identity Management and Federal Protective Service under NPPD continued to operate during the furlough, with funding made available through fee revenues and multi-year appropriations. Most of the Secret Service and NPPD cybersecurity function continued to work in the absence of annual appropriations because of Antideficiency Act exemptions.

As it faced the 2013 shutdown, DHS identified several activities that would be subject to furloughs and curtailment of activities under a lapse in annual appropriations, including all non-disaster grant programs, NPPD's Critical Infrastructure Protective Security Advisor Program, the Chemical Site Security Regulatory Program, and research and development activities. As the underlying laws that determine who is furloughed and who is exempt have not changed, one can expect a similar result in the event that fiscal year 2015 appropriations lapse.

I would like to thank the subcommittee again. Like all of us at the Congressional Research Service, I am happy to answer your questions.

[The prepared statement of Mr. Painter follows:]

PREPARED STATEMENT OF WILLIAM PAINTER

FEBRUARY 12, 2015

Good morning Chairman Ratcliffe, Ranking Member Richmond, and Members of the subcommittee.

I am privileged to appear before you today on behalf of CRS in response to your request to discuss how the budget situation for the Department of Homeland Security (DHS) could affect the efforts of its various components to develop new technologies and confront emerging threats.

Accordingly, my statement summarizes key portions of several CRS reports regarding DHS appropriations for fiscal year 2015, the impact of continuing resolutions (CRs), and the impact of a lapse in annual appropriations for DHS.

I will begin with a brief overview of the current status of the DHS appropriations process, and then discuss three potential scenarios and what each would entail for DHS developing technology and confronting emerging threats.

When discussing specific programs, I will explore the impact of various potential budget scenarios on the operations of the DHS components represented on the panel with me today, National Programs and Protection Directorate (NPPD), the Domestic Nuclear Detection Office (DNDO), the Science and Technology Directorate (S&T), and to a limited extent, the cybersecurity-related functions of the U.S. Secret Service (USSS). Unfortunately, the publicly-available documentation regarding the USSS budget lacks the granularity necessary to discuss those functions in significant detail.

DHS APPROPRIATIONS CURRENT STATUS

DHS operated with an overall budget of $59.2 billion for fiscal year 2014. Forty-seven-point-nine billion dollars, or 81%, was discretionary spending, which relied on budget authority provided through appropriations acts.[1] The fiscal year 2014 Homeland Security Appropriations Act (Pub. L. No. 113–76, Division F) enacted almost $3 billion for DNDO, S&T, and NPPD.

The administration requested $60.9 billion for DHS for fiscal year 2015, of which $49.0 billion was discretionary funding. DNDO, S&T, and NPPD comprised $2.9 billion of that request.

As fiscal year 2014 drew to a close, no annual appropriations bills for fiscal year 2015 had been enacted. On September 19, 2014, the President signed into law Pub. L. No. 113–164, which provided temporary funding for Government operations as senior appropriators indicated they would pursue an omnibus appropriations package in the closing months of the 113th Congress, rather than stand-alone appropriations bills. The Consolidated and Further Continuing Appropriations Act, 2015, was signed into law as Pub. L. No. 113–235 on December 16, 2014. Congress did not include full annual appropriations for DHS as part of the package, but provided an extension of continuing appropriations for the Department through February 27, 2015.[2]

The administration submitted its fiscal year 2016 budget request to Congress on February 2, 2015. According to the Department, the request includes almost $64.9 billion for DHS, more than $51.9 billion of which is discretionary spending. When compared in fiscal year 2015, this represents a $3.7 billion increase compared to the overall DHS budget request, and a $2.8 billion increase in the DHS discretionary request. The requested appropriations for NPPD, S&T, and DNDO total almost $2.8 billion.

The annual appropriation for DHS was not finalized when the budget request was assembled. DHS does not directly compare in its public budget request documentation the fiscal year 2016 request with the legislation under consideration for fiscal year 2015. Table 1 provides such a comparison for the selected agencies.

[1] Department of Homeland Security, *Budget in Brief, Fiscal Year 2016,* p. 8.
[2] Division L of Pub. L. No. 113–235.

TABLE 1.—ENACTED, REQUESTED, AND PROPOSED APPROPRIATIONS FOR SELECTED DHS COMPONENTS, FISCAL YEAR 2014– FISCAL YEAR 2016

(Budget Authority in Rounded Millions of Dollars)

Component/Appropriation	Fiscal Year 2014 Enacted	Fiscal Year 2015 Budget Request	Fiscal Year 2015 H.R. 240	Fiscal Year 2016 Budget Request	Analysis of Fiscal Year 2016 Request vs. H.R. 240 +/- $	Analysis of Fiscal Year 2016 Request vs. H.R. 240 +/- %
U.S. Secret Service (USSS):						
Salaries and expenses	$1,538	$1,586	$1,616	$1,867	$252	15.6%
Acquisition, construction, improvements, and related expenses ..	52	50	50	72	22	43.5%
USSS TOTAL	1,590	1,636	1,666	1,939	273	16.4%
National Protection and Programs Directorate (NPPD):						
Management and Administration	56	66	62	64	3	4.1%
Infrastructure Protection and Information Security	1,187	1198	1189	1,312	123	10.3%
Federal Protective Service (FPS)*	[1,302]	[1343]	[1343]	[1,443]	101	7.5%
Office of Biometric Identity Management	227	252	252	284	31	12.5%
NPPD TOTAL	1,471	1,515	1,502	1,659	157	10.5%
Science and Technology (S&T):						
Management and Administration	129	130	130	132	2	1.6%
Research, Development, and Operations	1,091	942	974	647	−327	−33.6%
S&T TOTAL	1,220	1,072	1,104	779	−325	−29.4%
Domestic Nuclear Detection Office (DNDO):						
Management and Administration	37	37	37	38	1	2.6%
Research, Development, and Operations	205	199	198	196	−2	−1.0%
Systems Acquisition	43	68	73	123	50	69.4%
DNDO TOTAL	285	304	308	357	49	16.1%

* FPS is not included in the total resources because it is funded through collections from the agencies for whom FPS provides services.

Sources.—CRS analysis of fiscal year 2014 explanatory statement, fiscal year 2015 DHS Congressional justifications, H.R. 240 (114th Congress), and the DHS Budget in Brief, Fiscal Year 2016.

Notes.—Table displays rounded numbers for simplicity of presentation. To ensure validity of analysis, all operations, including calculations of percentages, were performed with unrounded data.

The evolution of funding levels across the three fiscal years reflected in this chart (as well as other changes below the appropriations level that are not reflected here) could be taken as evidence that DHS and Congressional priorities in confronting emerging threats are evolving as well. The resolution of the fiscal year 2015 annual appropriations cycle will have a significant impact on the ability of the Department to align its funding to those new priorities. Budgets that are based on prior year funding streams or that are more procedurally limiting than the annual appropriations process could present additional challenges to the Department as it works to adjust to the evolving threat environment.

FISCAL YEAR 2015 DHS APPROPRIATIONS: POTENTIAL FUTURE SCENARIOS

At least three possible scenarios exist as the February 27 expiration date of the current DHS funding stream approaches:
  (1) extension of the continuing resolution;
  (2) enactment of a fiscal year 2015 annual appropriations bill for DHS; or
  (3) a lapse in discretionary appropriations.

EXTENSION OF THE CONTINUING RESOLUTION

Continuing resolutions (CRs)—the basis of the first possible scenario—come in two forms, distinguished by the duration of funding they provide. The most common type is an "interim" CR, which provides temporary funding for departments or agencies that lack enacted annual appropriations. Such finding is typically provided at a given rate for operations. This type of CR expires at a specified date prior to the end of the fiscal year. It may be extended through the enactment of further interim CRs, or superseded by annual appropriations laws. DHS has been operating under temporary CRs throughout fiscal year 2015, providing funding slightly less than the fiscal year 2014 rate for operations.

My colleagues have written extensively on the history, functions, and impacts of interim continuing resolutions, and I refer you to their work for detailed analysis.[3] Usually funding is provided to sustain a rate for operations defined in terms of funding enacted in the previous fiscal year. That rate may be adjusted by formula or by specific "anomalies"[4] on a pro-rated basis, which is calculated based on the CR's duration. Any obligations or expenditures that are made using this temporary funding are typically deducted from the applicable full-year appropriation once enacted.

The second type of CR is a "full-year" CR, which provides funding through the end of the fiscal year. DHS has operated under the terms of such a CR only once, in fiscal year 2011. That year, Congress agreed only on the budget for the Department of Defense. The rest of the Government operated under the terms of a full-year CR[5] from mid-April to the end of September, 2011. Defined funding levels (as opposed to a rate of operations) were established, and were generally the amounts in the previous fiscal year's appropriations laws (except when set by anomalies).

To preserve Congressional prerogatives, Congress generally places several key restrictions on the use of continuing funding under an interim CR. The current CR,[6] as amended, includes those traditional restrictions, including:
  • *Section 101(a).*—That appropriations are provided "under the authority and conditions" of the fiscal year 2014 appropriations laws, for projects or activities "that were conducted in fiscal year 2014", and that were funded in those specified appropriations acts;[7]
  • *Section 104.*—That funds may not be used to initiate or resume any project or activity not funded during fiscal year 2014;[8]
  • *Section 109.*—That funding distributions or grant awards shall not be made that would impinge on Congress's final funding prerogatives;[9] and

---

[3] For information on the history and procedural aspects of CRs, see CRS Report R42647, *Continuing Resolutions: Overview of Components and Recent Practices*, by Jessica Tollestrup; for information on the impacts of interim CRs, see CRS Report RL34700, *Interim Continuing Resolutions (CRs): Potential Impacts on Agency Operations*, by Clinton T. Brass.

[4] Anomalies are generally defined as provisions that alter the funding stream provided under a continuing resolution or the authorities under which that funding is utilized, i.e., increasing or decreasing the rate for operations for a specific program, barring the use of funds for a specific activity, or specifically authorizing an activity.

[5] Division B of Pub. L. No. 112–10.

[6] Pub. L. No. 113–164 as amended.

[7] 128 Stat 1867.

[8] 128 Stat 1868.

[9] 128 Stat 1869.

- *Section 110.*—That only the most limited funding action permitted in the resolution shall be made to continue projects and activities.[10]

The restrictions noted above in Sections 109 and 110 were not included in the fiscal year 2011 full-year CR, and the restrictions in Section 104 were modified, as the legislation was anticipated to be the final action on appropriations for the fiscal year.

An agency funded under an interim CR experiences several challenges in confronting a dynamic threat environment and developing new technologies. To some extent, a status quo funding level combined with the restrictions on the use of funds provided under the terms of a continuing resolution may result in Federal agencies continuing to support existing priorities—rather than shifting to new ones—since only existing programs retain funding.

In reports stretching back several years, the Government Accountability Office (GAO) has noted multiple negative effects of interim continuing resolutions on efficient program management and execution. GAO variously cited: The inability to allocate funds to programs with current needs, rather than a (possibly no longer relevant) recent history of funding; delays in planning; hiring freezes; delays in construction projects; suspension of loan and grant activities; inability to finalize or renew contracts in a timely manner; reductions in technical assistance work; delays in funding that increased program costs; and reductions in otherwise justifiable travel.[11]

Other observers concur that interim CRs can have negative impacts. Past reporting by CRS regarding the impacts of interim CRs on the Department of Defense noted that interim CRs create challenges in the distribution of funds, requiring an "inordinate amount of time and paper," and drawing resources from "more productive management." The reporting also noted that interim CRs do not provide the authority to reestablish bonuses and allowances for personnel, which can negatively affect morale and retention of highly sought-after personnel.[12]

If full-year regular appropriations levels for fiscal year 2015 become law, thereby allowing new programs to receive funds, projects may have difficulty meeting their projected time lines because of the shortened time frame for obligating funds for these programs. With the midpoint of the fiscal year approaching, difficulties may emerge in obligating some of the new appropriations for NPPD, for example, before they expire at the end of the fiscal year. Most of the budget for DNDO and S&T does not expire for 3 or 5 years; however, 81% of NPPD's Infrastructure Protection and Information Security appropriation in H.R. 240 expires at the end of fiscal year 2015.

One example of how either an interim or year-long CR that extends last year's funding levels with no anomalies[13] could affect DHS activities is the Chemical Facility Anti-Terrorism Standards (CFATS) activity at NPPD.

CFATS would be affected both in terms of its funding and its operations. In terms of funding, the Infrastructure Security Compliance Division (ISCD) requested an 8% increase in fiscal year 2015 from their appropriated level in fiscal year 2014 ($87 million as opposed to $81 million). In practice, DHS had reprogrammed an additional $3 million to ISCD in fiscal year 2014. Under a clean CR, ISCD would be funded at a lower level than required to provide current services.

In terms of operations, in December 2014, ISCD received new statutory authorization to regulate chemical facilities for security purposes. The new authority contains new provisions for ISCD to implement, including increased information sharing, the commission of certain studies, and the establishment of a self-certification program for regulated entities. Not all of these activities were in place in fiscal year 2014. The costs of implementing them would not be represented in a funding stream based on fiscal year 2014 funding, and DHS may consider some of them as new activities that could not be initiated under the continuing resolution.

Another potential effect of a CR that extended fiscal year 2014 levels would be on the S&T Laboratory Facilities appropriation. In fiscal year 2014, the construction of the National Bio- and Agro-defense Facility received $404 million in appropriations. The request for fiscal year 2015 was $300 million, which was included in both the House and Senate draft bills in the previous Congress and in H.R. 240. Despite what appears as consensus on a funding level, a CR at fiscal year 2014 levels would provide more for NBAF construction than either Congress or the administration have proposed.

---

[10] Ibid.

[11] Summarized in CRS Report RL34700, *Interim Continuing Resolutions (CRs): Potential Impacts on Agency Operations*, by Clinton T. Brass.

[12] Ibid.

[13] In practice, interim and full-year CRs usually contain at least some anomalies.

DNDO's Human Portable Radiation Detection Systems program would have the opposite issue. This program purchases commercially-available technology for front-line DHS personnel to detect radiological or nuclear materials in the field. The fiscal year 2015 request of $51 million was almost triple the fiscal year 2014 funding level of $14 million. Again, the House and Senate generally concurred on providing most of the increase, but an anomaly would be required to provide that increase if the CR generally extended the fiscal year 2014 funding level.

Given the structure of appropriations for S&T, funding shifts below the level of the Project, Program, and Activity level are common. Such shifts can provide the resources needed to carry out work under existing authorities. However, given the level of budget uncertainty, even in cases where S&T has the legal ability to engage in new work, there may be a hesitancy to make a commitment of resources when operating under a temporary CR.

ENACTMENT OF FISCAL YEAR 2015 ANNUAL APPROPRIATIONS

The second potential next scenario—enactment of an annual appropriations bill—would arguably allow DHS to carry out its mission with more transparent and explicit direction from Congress in terms of funding levels and funding limitations for many of its missions. DHS may perceive more freedom to engage in certain activities, such as the hiring of staff. It would also be able to initiate certain new projects, as is the case for the other Government agencies funded through the consolidated appropriations act enacted in December, 2014.

For the purposes of discussion, let us assume that the annual appropriation includes the funding levels outlined in H.R. 240, the fiscal year 2015 Homeland Security Appropriations bills introduced in the House in the 114th Congress.

Under the terms of H.R. 240, in fiscal year 2015, DNDO would receive an almost 8% increase overall above fiscal year 2014. A $7 million reduction in the Research Development and Operations account would be offset by an increase of $35 million in the Human Portable Radiation Detection Program. While $2 million less than requested by the administration, the resources provided would still support the purchase of portable radiation detectors for Customs and Border Protection, the Transportation Security Administration, and the U.S. Coast Guard.

S&T would be funded $116 million below fiscal year 2014 levels under H.R. 240 as passed by the House. The major driver in this reduction is the smaller tranche of funding for the construction of the National Bio- and Agrodefense Facility. A 1% reduction in the Research, Development, and Innovation subappropriation also is present. As with DNDO, the funding levels included in the two bills are higher than the administration's request for fiscal year 2015.

In House-passed H.R. 240, NPPD would be funded at slightly more than $1.5 billion—almost $32 million above the fiscal year 2014 level, and $13 million below the administration's request. Most of the increase from the previous fiscal year is driven by a $32 million increase in the Next Generation Networks program and rejection of an $8 million proposed reduction in the Global Cybersecurity Management subappropriation. This would maintain funding levels for cybersecurity education.

The explanatory statement for H.R. 240 notes that USSS "cyber activities, including electronic crimes investigations and State and local cyber crime training" would receive more than $108 million under the terms of H.R. 240. A similar figure was not presented in the explanatory statement for the fiscal year 2014 appropriation to allow for definitive overall comparison, although the support for training rose from $7.5 million in the fiscal year 2014 act to $12 million in H.R. 240.

POTENTIAL FISCAL YEAR 2015 FUNDING LAPSE FOR DHS

The third scenario—a default option which will occur if neither of the first two scenarios occur—is a lapse in annual appropriations for the Department. DHS will be required to implement a shutdown furlough. The events of October 2013 provide a reasonable understanding of this case. The shutdown affected operations of different DHS components to varying degrees. Roughly 85% of the Department's workforce continued with their duties during the shutdown, because of exceptions identified in long-standing interpretations of the Anti-Deficiency Act. Some DHS employees were also recalled to work after the furloughs began on the basis of unanticipated needs (such as disaster response activities) and the enactment of an appropriations law that temporarily covered certain personnel costs.

In the event of a lapse, DHS personnel who continue to work without passage of annual appropriations or a continuing resolution generally fall into two categories: Those whose activities are not funded through 1-year appropriations, and those whose work is necessary for the preservation of the safety of human life or the protection of property. The former generally continue to be paid as scheduled—contingent on the availability of funds, whereas the latter are not paid while the lapse in annual appropriations continues. Of DHS's estimated 231,117 civilian and military employees, nearly 200,000 were projected to be exempted from the shutdown furlough, according to the Department. Most of these employees relied on annual appropriations for their salaries, and therefore were not paid during the funding lapse.

Among the components of interest today, only the Office of Biometric Identity Management and Federal Protective Service under NPPD continued to operate during the furlough with funding made available through fee revenues and multi-year appropriations. Elements of the Secret Service engaged in protection of persons and facilities and NPPD's cybersecurity function continued to work in the absence of annual appropriations.

Table 2 provides a breakdown of the initial exemption and furlough data provided by DHS for the four components under discussion:[14]

TABLE 2.—DHS PROJECTED INITIAL EXEMPTION AND FURLOUGH DATA FOR SELECTED COMPONENTS, FISCAL YEAR 2014 LAPSE

Component	Employees (as of 7/31/2013)	Projected Exempt	Projected Furlough	Projected % of Component Furloughed
U.S. Secret Service	6,537	6,003	534	8.17%
National Protection and Programs Directorate	2,835	1,617	1,218	42.96%
Science and Technology Directorate	469	20	449	95.74%
Domestic Nuclear Detection Office	115	6	109	94.78%

Source.—CRS analysis of DHS "Procedures Relating to a Federal Funding Hiatus," September 27, 2013.

While DHS did not associate numbers of furloughed employees with specific programs, the Department identified several activities that would be subject to furloughs and curtailment of activities, including:

- all non-disaster grant programs;
- NPPD's Critical Infrastructure Protective Security Advisor Program;
- chemical site security regulatory program; and
- research and development activities.[15]

Most of the research and development activities funded by S&T and DNDO are performed by contractors. Even if its work was funded prior to the shutdown, a contractor might be prevented from continuing its work if it required access to a closed DHS facility or interaction with a furloughed DHS employee. If the shutdown persisted for an extended period, some contractors might suspend their work because of uncertainty or cash flow issues.[16]

One difference from the consequences of the fiscal year 2013 shutdown would be in the CFATS program. Since DHS has received new statutory authority to regulate chemical facility security,[17] the statute underlying chemical facility security regulation would remain in force. The previous authority had a sunset date that was typically extended each year in appropriations acts. In the prior shutdown, DHS furloughed the staff of ISCD, which implements the program. If ISCD staff were again furloughed, the regulatory program they implement would pause, even though the statutory authority would continue in force.

A lapse in annual appropriation and the shutdown furlough that would follow could represent a disruption in certain DHS operations, and potentially raise more obstacles to efficient management and oversight than those raised by an interim continuing resolution.

I would be remiss if I did not close by noting that while I sit before you today, the testimony I have provided would not have been possible without the contribu-

---

[14] A complete breakdown of DHS projected furloughs is available in CRS Report R43252, *FY2014 Appropriations Lapse and the Department of Homeland Security: Impact and Legislation*, by William L. Painter.

[15] "DHS Lapse Contingency Plan Summary," September 27, 2013. Provided by DHS Legislative Affairs.

[16] For additional information on how contracted work may be affected by a lapse in annual appropriations, see CRS Report WSLG681, *What Would a Government Shutdown Mean for Federal Contractors?*, by Kate M. Manuel.

[17] Pub. L. No. 113-254.

tions of a number of my colleagues as well, especially Clinton Brass, Jessica Tollestrup, Dana Shea, Daniel Morgan, John Moteff, and Eric Fisher.

On behalf of CRS, thank you for the opportunity of appearing before you today. I am happy to respond to your questions.

Mr. RATCLIFFE. Thank you, Mr. Painter.

I now recognize myself for 5 minutes for questions.

Just a few days ago, President Obama announced the creation of the Cyber Threat and Intelligence Integration Center, or CTIIC, which will fall under the Office of the Director of National Intelligence. The stated purpose of this new center will be to integrate the intelligence community's cyber data and share it with civilian agencies.

Mr. Ozment, I would like to start with you and ask if you can discuss how DHS's NCCIC anticipates working with this new center. Specifically, what do you anticipate the roles and responsibilities will be for each?

Mr. OZMENT. Thank you, Chairman.

As you know, NPPD and the NCCIC are not a part of the intelligence community, nor is NPPD's NCCIC a law enforcement organization. The CTIIC, the Cyber Threat Intelligence Integration Center, is designed to address a specific problem: The integration of intelligence from across intelligence community agencies.

From the perspective to the NCCIC, the CTIIC will be a supporting organization. The NCCIC is one of the operational cybersecurity organizations, along with NCIJTF, the National Cyber Joint Investigative Task Force, and U.S. Cyber Command's Joint Operations Center.

The CTIIC will provide integrated intelligence in support of the NCCIC's daily operations. From that perspective, the CTIIC will help the NCCIC by providing that integrated perspective.

Mr. RATCLIFFE. Thank you, Mr. Ozment.

A question for you, Mr. Martin. In the past month, S&T has published its visionary goals. You mentioned those five today in your testimony. Is it S&T's intention to shape its research agenda to align with these visionary goals? If so, what do you envision as the right mix between basic research and the applied science and engineering?

Mr. MARTIN. Thank you, Chairman.

It is the intention of the Directorate to shape its portfolio based on these visionary goals. It is going to be a split between research and development done to support the operational needs of the component and a portion of the portfolio to go towards Apex programs, which are mapped to these visionary goals.

Our Apex programs take a more focused view at some pretty critical problems in the Department. It is a mixture of both basic and applied research. I can't give you exact amounts because it depends on the maturity of the technology we are looking at.

Ultimately, we want to have a relatively good mix of both basic and applied research.

Mr. RATCLIFFE. Thank you, Mr. Martin.

Dr. Gowadia, a question for you. Currently, as you know, DHS is required by the SAFE Port Act to scan 100 percent of containerized cargo at foreign ports of departure before that is loaded onto ships coming to the United States. Currently, DHS has requested waivers since 2012 because it has been unable to reach that goal.

I want to know, do you think that, given that the Secretary has requested these multiple waivers, is this law even feasible, No. 1? No. 2, what are some of the recommendations that you have for addressing the threat at foreign ports of departure?

Ms. GOWADIA. Thank you, Chairman Ratcliffe.

At the Department, we share your concern about the threat of the use of a cargo container bringing a nuclear material to our ports, and we have remained committed to make sure that goods that arrive here are safe and secure before they are released into the American public.

Our Secretary has directed us to take another look at the 100 percent overseas scanning mandate, and so we are doing that in concert with our industry partners as well as with foreign governments. This mandate cannot, of course, be implemented without their engagement. We need to find a business model that works for all of us to that end.

Also, DNDO has a fairly significant role to play, and we collaborate with S&T to make sure that we are developing the right technologies to be able to address this mandate.

That having been said, let me reassure you, sir, that 100 percent of cargo containers are scanned at our ports of entry before they are released into the stream of commerce right here in the United States.

So we are looking at this layered, disciplined approach to attack the problem.

Mr. RATCLIFFE. Terrific. Thank you, Dr. Gowadia.

Mr. Noonan, very quickly in my time remaining, can you address Secret Service's relationship with DHS, with the NCCIC, and how all that comes into play when investigating cyber breaches?

Mr. NOONAN. Yes, sir.

As a matter of practice over the last several years, when we are engaged in a cyber investigation and we are working together with a private-sector victim, we have our forensic specialists that are working with that victim company, and we are pulling out of those investigations evidence that is important in that investigation.

When we pull out evidence in that investigation, we also see the criminal tools that the criminal uses to gain access and entry into those systems, we see the malicious code that they use to insert in those systems. When these things are new trends that we are observing, we take that information that we glean out of that criminal investigation and we share that with our partners at the DHS's NCCIC.

DHS's NCCIC, together with the Secret Service, will put together a product. When we put this product together, we are very concerned about the privacy of the victim company, so we strip out everything related back to that company. We share those cybersecurity matters through the NCCIC out to the rest of infrastructure.

As a matter of fact, because US–CERT sits with the NCCIC, US–CERT also pumps that same information out to the rest of a number of CERTs around the globe, too. So we are getting those cybersecurity concerns not just out to the critical infrastructure here domestically, but we are also getting out to our partners out there outside the borders of the United States to better protect their systems from our criminal adversaries that are taking advantage of our financial systems.

Mr. RATCLIFFE. Thank you, Mr. Noonan.

My time has expired. The Chairman now recognizes the Ranking Minority Member, Mr. Richmond, for his questions.

Mr. RICHMOND. Thank you, Mr. Chairman. I am going to yield my time to the Ranking Member of the full committee, Mr. Thompson.

Mr. THOMPSON. Thank you very much, Mr. Richmond.

We have had some very interesting testimony here today. There is no question that cyber is a clear and present priority as well as a danger for us as American citizens.

One of the things I want to highlight, though, is that if we don't have a Department that is funded, a lot of the missions we have talked about here today will suffer. So what I want to give my time toward is to further elaborate on that 16-day window that we are facing in terms of not having a funded Department of Homeland Security.

Mr. Painter, you gave us three scenarios. I think all of them, under any circumstance, gives pause for a Department that really needs to get about its business of securing this country.

What I am really concerned about, though, is the shutdown possibility and what that does for us. Are you saying that S&T would be one of those departments that would be impacted disproportionately to others in terms of employees that would be sent home?

Mr. PAINTER. Thank you for the question, Ranking Member Thompson.

The analysis that was included in my testimony was based on the shutdown furlough plan that was released for the October 2013 shutdown. As we approach the possibility of a lapse in appropriations, the Department will release a similar plan that will outline exactly how many employees are in each section and who is likely to be furloughed.

However, one thing that the Department made clear in its plan in 2013 and has been discussed is that the research and development activities are not considered exempt under the Antideficiency Act, and, therefore, those activities would be shut down.

Mr. THOMPSON. Thank you.

Mr. Noonan, there is no question that our men and women in the Secret Service do a wonderful job. We have been more than supportive as a committee, but there are about 4,000 agents who would be impacted if we don't have a budget at the end of this month.

In your opinion, what effect would that have on the morale of those men and women?

Mr. NOONAN. Thank you for the question, sir.

I think a CR will inherently slow down the execution and day-to-day operations of the Secret Service as it relates to our cyber program. It will delay hiring. It will impact our operations.

I think along with that, you know, I think the men and women of the Secret Service are very dedicated to their mission. At the end of day, we will get our mission done. But, to your point, I think there will be a—obviously, there will be some impact, of course.

Mr. THOMPSON. So the best way to get on with our challenge is to have a budget so that we know how to plan and implement accordingly. Thank you.

Dr. Ozment, how is the implementation of CFATS impacted by this potential shutdown or lack of moneys for the Department?

Mr. OZMENT. Ranking Member, I am here today to represent NPPD. I will tell you, however, that I am the lead of our cybersecurity programs, and, therefore, I am not confident that I could give you the depth of answer that I would like to give you on the CFATS program. So I will ask if we can respond to your staff in more detail on that later.

If you are interested, however, I am happy to talk to you about its impact on our cybersecurity programs.

Mr. THOMPSON. Go on.

Mr. OZMENT. Thank you, Ranking Member.

Mr. THOMPSON. But get me the other information, too.

Mr. OZMENT. Absolutely, sir.

Mr. THOMPSON. Okay.

Mr. OZMENT. I am gravely concerned about the impact of a shutdown on our cybersecurity efforts. NPPD will experience three categories of significant impacts to our cybersecurity mission if there is a shut down: To our operations, to our key acquisition programs, and to our information-sharing activities.

First, a shutdown will cause us to lose the support of over 140 staff in our NCCIC. Without these staff, the NCCIC's capacity to provide a timely response to agencies or critical-infrastructure customers seeking assistance after a cybersecurity incident will be decreased, and we will be less able to conduct expedited technical analysis of cybersecurity threats.

Second, a shutdown will delay two acquisition programs that are essential to protecting Federal agencies from cybersecurity attacks and intrusions.

First is the National Cybersecurity Protection System, otherwise known as EINSTEIN. We are currently ready to bring on board new agencies for the protection of EINSTEIN 3. A shutdown would prevent us from bringing on board those agencies and essentially stop those agencies from receiving the protection that they need from the cyber threats that are out there.

In addition, the Continuous Diagnostics and Mitigation Program is on the verge of issuing a contract that will allow Federal agencies to identify critical cyber vulnerabilities and expedite their resolution. A shutdown would delay the issuance of this award and again leave agencies unprotected and less able to patch and be even cognizant of the vulnerabilities that they have.

The final category of significant impacts would be to our information-sharing activities. A shutdown would significantly reduce the volume and timeliness of cyber threat information that we are able to share with our Government partners and the private sector. We will also be unable to bring on board new companies as partners in information sharing and will be unable to continue planning our next-generation information-sharing capabilities that are necessary to make our information sharing real-time and automated in order to enable us to combat highly-sophisticated cyber threats.

Mr. THOMPSON. Thank you very much, Mr. Chairman, and I appreciate your indulgence in allowing the question to be answered. I yield back.

Mr. RATCLIFFE. You are welcome.

The gentleman's time has expired.

The Chairman now recognizes the Ranking Minority Member and gentleman from Louisiana, Mr. Richmond.

Mr. RICHMOND. Thank you, Mr. Chairman.

I will start with Dr. Gowadia, and I will continue where the Ranking Member left off, which is, in the next 16 days, if we don't do something to fund long-term the Department of Homeland Security, how would that affect the work that the Domestic Nuclear Detection Office does with local law enforcement agencies as far as the alerts go?

Ms. GOWADIA. Thank you, Mr. Richmond.

As far as responding to the alerts and alarms that come up from our operational partners, we have actually established that particular function as a mission-essential function. So, with a skeletal staff, we will be able to support and answer those phone calls, but it will be only with 10 civilian personnel and about 5 military detailees. So it will be a tremendous burden on the staff, sir.

Mr. RICHMOND. Now, let's talk about your fiscal year 2015 and 2016 budgets as far as acquisitions go. If we decrease your budget for next year, how would that affect your acquisitions?

Ms. GOWADIA. As you are aware, sir, we are a mission support office. We buy detectors for our Customs and Border Protection colleagues, TSA, Coast Guard. The big difference between the 2014 budget and the 2015 budget, the President's request, is a $37 million plug to get us in a position to buy handheld detectors and identification systems for deployment in the field.

Very specifically, the detectors that our CBP colleagues have today are no longer supported by the vendor and have reached the end of their service life. We need to replace them so that we can make sure that commerce is not held up at the ports while we wait to get the right detection technologies to bear.

It is a tremendous operational burden on our CBP colleagues, and so this is much-needed funds to make sure that they are able to exercise their duties in the field.

Mr. RICHMOND. Which is very important to me and the district I represent, considering that we have the Port of New Orleans, Port of South Louisiana, Port of Baton Rouge, that, if you add them up and make them one port complex, we are probably No. 3 in the world, No. 1 in the United States.

As we continue to push trade and looming trade deals in front of us, then this would be one example of really pushing a trade deal but not putting the funds in a place to make sure that we can get goods to commerce in a quick and orderly fashion.

Mr. Martin, let me ask you almost the same question, that if you don't have long-term funding or anticipated funding, what do you think the long-term effects would be to the S&T and First Responder programs, No. 1, if we fail to fund DHS; No. 2, if we cut the budget?

Mr. MARTIN. Ranking Member Richmond, in a word, it is disruptive. It is disruptive in the short term in that we can't do the support work for the State and local first responders that we do. It also puts a level of uncertainty in our research and development. It is very difficult to turn research and development on and off.

It is also very difficult to start and stop contracts that do a lot of our research work. Probably one of the longer-term effects of this is we lose confidence of small business, of universities, of National labs to do work with the Federal Government. If we can't have stable budgets and sustained funding to support these programs, we lose the confidence of those groups to do work with us.

From the first-responder perspective, it is going to be difficult for us to maintain any level of direct support for equipment testing, for any type of research or knowledge products we develop to move to them. To be able to keep that level of confidence in the responders of the work we do requires a stable budget.

Mr. RICHMOND. Then I guess the common theme I am hearing is that, although we would not fund you all and you all would be disrupted and you would make do the best you can, the local law enforcement agencies around the country, the State and locals, would really be, for lack of a better description, left out there on their own because they can't rely on your support and help that you normally offer them.

So, with that, Mr. Chairman, I would just like to say that I think that, you know, it is very critical that we fund it. I know that both sides differ much on immigration, and we will fight on immigration, and it is a legitimate difference of opinion. But I think that their testimony highlights the fact that we should not jeopardize the safety of the country over that one fight, which we will continue to embark on.

So, with that, Mr. Chairman, thank you for your time, and I yield back.

Mr. RATCLIFFE. The Chairman thanks the gentleman.

The Chairman will now recognize other Members of the subcommittee for questions they may wish to ask the witnesses.

I would like to recognize the gentleman from Florida, Mr. Clawson.

Mr. CLAWSON. Thank you.

Thanks for coming, you all. I am always appreciative for folks who show up and have to get in the middle of our big battles that we have up here.

You know, I have spent a lot of time in boardrooms, not a lot of time in these committees meetings. You know, I was always surprised—the way we do things, the witnesses come, they get in the middle of this partisan bashing. So if they get the wrong question, they don't want to answer it because it will make their side look bad; if they get the right question, then they want to answer. Then we just dig the divide between the two sides bigger and bigger. We don't learn anything as a result of that because we have a hard time getting to full disclosure because we are too busy being partisan.

I fly over that, or at least I try to. I appreciate you all coming today. I hope you will be as open as we can because I don't want to pick a partisan bone here. I think it is a waste of time. We will have that fight another day, and that will be a different conversation.

But I did want to pick your brain about a couple of things that I am interested in as I did the study here. It feels blurry to me on where the line is between private companies, private data, private people, and our own defense of cybersecurity. So I am curious, you know, how many different agencies get involved with our private companies? What are the limits of that? What is the kind of data that our Federal agencies should be asking for?

If you put yourself in the position of somebody who is running a company, who has fiduciary responsibility not just to the community but also the privacy of customers, employees, fiduciary responsibility to shareholders, kind-of, what is the right answer to all that? As the stakes get higher here and we get more and more unsafe, who gets to decide?

So two or three of you I am sure have strong opinions on this, and I would objectively just like your objective viewpoint on it. Whoever would like to start first, I would really like it.

Mr. NOONAN. Yes, sir.

As far as law enforcement goes and working with our private-sector partners, it is really a two-way street of working with the victim company. A lot of times, it is the Secret Service and/or law enforcement that goes to the private sector when there is an incident, when there is a data breach, and we are the ones actually giving them information about the data breach and showing them where that data breach is.

Mr. CLAWSON. What if it is not somebody who has been a victim? I mean, don't we involve companies on a broad scale for prevention?

Mr. NOONAN. Absolutely. So, As a matter of fact, we are partnered with private-sector partners through our Electronic Crimes Task Forces. In those Electronic Crimes Task Forces, we have quarterly meetings with the private sector, and we share ideas on criminal trends, on how to better protect themselves——

Mr. CLAWSON. Is that mandatory participation?

Mr. NOONAN. Not on the private sector's part. On the Government's part, it is.

Mr. CLAWSON. What percentage of our private sector participates? Is it enough to really make a dent on this for what you all are trying to accomplish?

Mr. NOONAN. So, as it relates to our Electronic Crimes Task Forces, it depends on the city that we are in. There is no mandatory requirement, of course, for the private sector to belong to those.

In addition to that, we also send out industry notices to the private sector to better help them defend themselves from what we are seeing as the critical threat or the brand-new threat that is coming out and arising in those situations.

Mr. CLAWSON. If you had to grade the private sector, 1 to 10, about the kind of cooperation and participation that you are getting for disaster prevention, what would you give the grade?

Mr. NOONAN. I would give it a rather high grade as far as working in the financial services sector in relation to the work with law enforcement in prevention of those different matters that you just brought up.

Mr. CLAWSON. In other industries?

Mr. NOONAN. In other industries—I am not too involved with many other industries. The retail sector, obviously, over the last year, has become more engaged in information sharing with law enforcement and more engaged with the Government in that fashion.

Mr. CLAWSON. Dr. Ozment.

Mr. OZMENT. Thank you, Congressman.

To your beginning point, I think it is worth noting that cybersecurity is one of the critical threats our Nation will face in the 21st Century. Given that, I believe almost every Government department and agency will ultimately have a role in cybersecurity as their traditional work moves on-line and every agency has to work with the private sector as they normally engage.

So you will see, as you already do, the Secret Service engaging in electronic crimes, cybersecurity in their law enforcement capacity; sector-specific agencies, like the Department of Energy or Treasury, engaging with the sectors that they engage with, focusing on helping them in their cybersecurity; and, of course, the Department of Homeland Security looking at cross-sectors, trying to build the security and resilience of the American economy and our critical infrastructure.

I would like to highlight—you mentioned concerns about the protection of private-sector information—that the Department has a Congressionally-legislated program called Protected Critical Infrastructure Information, or PCII. Organizations, companies that share information with the NCCIC, for example, that request PCII protections are protected against civil litigation, Freedom of Information Act laws at either the Federal or State level, and from the disclosure of that information to their regulators.

We have many information-sharing partners and many companies who are participating, increasing the National security, and also helping each other and themselves by being a part of information-sharing efforts.

Nonetheless, I think it is important that we pass additional cybersecurity information-sharing legislation. The administration's cyber threat indicator sharing proposal is carefully tailored to ensure that privacy and civil liberties are protected while getting the very tactical threat information that we need to protect ourselves and our companies and our economy to the folks that need to use it to protect themselves.

Mr. CLAWSON. I hope we can have on-going conversations so that we can get the right balance here, because it very much concerns me that we will overreact and that individual customers and companies and folks will bear the price for that.

I yield back since I am over time. Sorry about that.

Mr. RATCLIFFE. The gentleman's time has expired, but I thank the gentleman from Florida.

I would also like to thank our panel of witnesses for your very valuable testimony. I would like to thank the Members present for their questions.

I know that some Members of the subcommittee may have additional questions for the witnesses, but we are about to be called to vote, and I know that we have some events after the vote that would preclude continuing the hearing. So, instead, we will ask you to respond to any questions in writing. Pursuant to the committee rule 7(e), the hearing record will be held open for 10 days.

Without objection, the subcommittee stands adjourned.

[Whereupon, at 4:00 p.m., the subcommittee was adjourned.]

APPENDIX

QUESTIONS FROM RANKING MEMBER BENNIE G. THOMPSON FOR ANDY OZMENT

Question 1a. Please describe the status and activities of the CFATS regulatory program under the second and third budget funding scenarios given by CRS testimony today. In other words, describe in detail all the activities, new or continuing, that would be curtailed, or not curtailed under:
Another CR, or short-term funding, and
Question 1b. Under a DHS-wide or Government-wide shut down.
Please include detailed metrics.

Answer. Prior to the *Protecting and Securing Chemical Facilities from Terrorist Attacks Act of 2014* (the CFATS Act of 2014), the Chemical Facility Anti-Terrorism Standards (CFATS) program was authorized through the appropriations process; accordingly, when the Federal Government faced a funding hiatus in 2013, the Department's authority to implement the Chemical Facility Anti-Terrorism Standards lapsed as well. It is not clear whether, had it been necessary, the Department would have had the authority to take enforcement action during the period of this lapse. With the enactment of the CFATS Act of 2014, the uncertainty surrounding the Department's authority has been lifted. Regardless of whether the employees responsible for administering the program would have been furloughed in the event of a funding lapse this year, facilities with approved security plans in place would have been required to implement those plans.

Had DHS not received funding and if the majority of CFATS program employees had been furloughed, the CFATS program might have seen an adverse impact to several high-priority activities. The program is currently working through a backlog of unapproved Site Security Plans, and a temporary stop to the CFATS program might have negatively impacted the number of facilities that would have been approved and therefore legally obligated to implement their security plans. For every week that CFATS inspection and Site-Security-Plan review activities might have ceased to occur during a funding hiatus, 20–30 additional high-risk chemical facilities that might otherwise have been required to implement anti-terrorism security measures might have gone unprotected against terrorist attack. Additionally, for every week of a shut down, DHS might have been unable to authorize approximately 35 to 40 security plans, conduct approximately 25 to 30 inspections of high-risk facilities, or issue nearly 30 final tiering letters.

A shut down might also have delayed the work being done to achieve the deadlines laid out in the CFATS Act, including the development of an outreach plan to identify potentially high-risk facilities that have not complied with their obligations under CFATS, whistleblower protection measures, and guidance for the regulated community on the Expedited Approval Program. Other impacts might have included delays to the development of information-sharing tools for first responders being created as part of Executive Order 13650, delays in rulemaking work being done to update the CFATS program, and delays in efforts to make improvements to the CFATS risk-tiering methodology.

QUESTIONS FROM HON. JAMES R. LANGEVIN FOR ANDY OZMENT

Question 1a. Signature-based threat detection is, by its very nature, reactive. Using robust information sharing and a broad network of intrusion detection and prevention systems, DHS can help ensure that exploits directed at Federal networks are one-offs—that is, they can't be reused. However, discovering the initial zero-day that a nation-state adversary or cyber terrorist uses against us presents a different problem. The incorporation of threat intelligence from the IC into E3A (Einstein 3 Accelerated) is one way to expand the base of threat indicators, but even E3A is only as good as the information it is fed.
How is NPPD addressing this challenge?

(53)

Answer. DHS intends to detect and block threats using three legs of a stool: Signature-based systems to block threats, analysis systems to identify new threats, and information sharing to disseminate threat information and to gather information for analysis.

As you note, intrusion detection and prevention systems are only as good as the information they have about "bad" traffic, which is recorded as "signatures." Signature-based systems are a necessary tool: Once we know about a threat, we use signature-based systems to block it rapidly and in a way that can scale across the whole Government. While signature-based tools are necessary, they are not sufficient. As you note, to detect and defend zero-day threats, we also must be able to detect new threats, traffic, or access that we don't already know is "bad." Those capabilities are built into our plans for the National Cybersecurity Protection System (NCPS), of which EINSTEIN 3 Accelerated (E3A) is one part.

The second leg of the stool is analysis. We will combine into NCPS the information that we gather from EINSTEIN 1, EINSTEIN 2, and EINSTEIN 3 with information that we will obtain from other programs like Continuous Diagnostics and Mitigation (CDM), other Government agencies, and information shared by the private sector. We will then use "big data analytics" to look at that information, identify anomalies and patterns, and detect new threats. Once we have identified previously-unknown threats, we will create signatures and push them out to E3A to block those threats. To complement this big data analytics approach, we are also exploring options to build adaptive analysis solutions into E3A itself, as described in the response to the next question.

The third leg of the stool is information sharing. When we learn about new threats, we will push the corresponding cyber threat indicators out to other Government agencies and the private sector in near-real time: At machine speed. By sharing these indicators, we will greatly reduce the likelihood that an adversary can re-use attack infrastructure, tools, tactics, techniques, and procedures. This means we increase the adversary cost, and decrease the likelihood, of successful attacks.

Our vision of a "weather map" describes this planned approach—and we are already in the process of implementing this vision. The vision includes: (1) Bringing together into NCPS the data from the EINSTEIN sensors, CDM, our Government partners, and information shared by the private sector; (2) visualizing that data to aid in situational awareness and analysis; (3) analyzing that data to detect and potentially anticipate malicious actors, and (4) sharing the resulting cyber threat indicators back to our Government partners and the private sector, thus creating a virtuous circle. As in all of our activities, we will incorporate the strong privacy and civil liberties protections and oversight that are already described in our Privacy Impact Assessments, which are publicly available at *dhs.gov*.

Question 1b. Are there other paradigms for detection that don't rely on foreknowledge of a threat?

Answer. Threat actors continually modify their attacks and are using increasingly targeted, clandestine, and dedicated techniques. As a result, we must build upon our signature-based approaches with solutions that will detect previously-unknown malicious activity. One solution as described in the response to the previous question, is to use big data analytics. In addition, we are currently exploring options to build non-signature based capabilities into E3A.

The Advanced Countermeasures and Automated Analytics Project utilizes the E3A Traffic Aggregation service to offer capabilities that blend speed and flexibility to detect advanced cyber threats, execute countermeasures to stop those threats from reaching their target, and increase the real-time and rich information sharing with departments and agencies. (E3A offers two services: Traffic Aggregation and Intrusion Prevention Security Service.)

This prototype uses computational intelligence algorithms and automated detection methods to identify and quantify anomalous behaviors, and employs tools and techniques to support threat-driven pattern recognition and "learning" algorithms.

Question 2a. I believe that convening stakeholders to help establish standards and encourage their adoption is an excellent way to leverage Federal investments in improving cybersecurity practices. DHS has played a vital role in the development of the STIX/TAXII system and in the deployment of the NIST Cybersecurity Framework (through the C3 Voluntary Program).

How can DHS continue to build upon these successes?

Answer. Voluntary cybersecurity standards and guidance through non-regulatory agencies such as NIST help private-sector entities to improve their own security.

DHS's Critical Infrastructure Cyber Community (C3, pronounced "C-Cubed") Voluntary Program is an innovative public-private partnership led by DHS as part of its continuing outreach and collaboration with the civilian government, State, local, Tribal, and territorial (SLTT) partners. The C3 Voluntary Program helps to align critical infrastructure owners and operators with existing resources that assist their efforts to manage their cyber risks, including through the use of the Cybersecurity Framework. It also facilitates forums for knowledge sharing and collaboration; provides access to free and readily-available technical assistance, tools, and resources to strengthen capabilities to manage cyber risks; and offers opportunities to exchange opinions with peers and other partners in the critical infrastructure community.

For the past 3 years, DHS has led the development in collaboration with the private sector of specifications—known as STIX and TAXII—which standardize the representation and exchange of cyber threat information, including actionable cyber threat indicators. STIX, the Structured Threat Information eXpression is a standardized format for the representation and exchange of cyber threat information, including indicators. TAXII, the Trusted Automated eXchange of Indicator Information, is a standardized protocol for discovering and exchanging cyber threat intelligence in STIX.

As you note, the STIX data format and the TAXII transport method are increasingly compatible with commonly-used commercial information technology (IT) products including platforms, network protection appliances, and endpoint security tools.

The Enhance Shared Situational Awareness (ESSA) initiative has chosen STIX as the basis for sharing cyber threat indicators between the Federal cyber centers, ensuring interoperability between these key sources of information. While the NCCIC has in-house systems and tools to assist analysts in generating STIX indicators, those indicators are currently analyzed and filtered by human analysts and shared back out with the private sector and Federal partners through manual methods such as e-mail and secure portals.

In 2014, the National Cybersecurity and Communications Integration Center (NCCIC) began a limited pilot with several organizations to test automated delivery of STIX indicators via TAXII and is currently executing a number of activities to expand automated cyber threat indicator-sharing capabilities. This means more entities are able to send indicators automatically to the NCCIC, creating an ecosystem of indicators which will in turn provide greater context to malicious cyber activity and rapidly increase situational awareness.

Intentionally adaptable, the Cybersecurity Framework and the STIX/TAXII protocols reflect a commitment to empowering Government and private-sector entities to manage and mitigate their own cybersecurity risks, with DHS as a coordination point and resource. DHS's NCCIC has a unique role as the center of integration, a hub for information sharing and collaborative analysis of global cyber risks, trends, and incidents.

Our leadership role lies in protecting civilian government systems and helping the private sector protect itself. In the future, we look to make tailored information sharing as effective as possible through voluntary collaboration. DHS looks to continue to correlate data from diverse sources in an anonymized and secure manner, to maximize insights and inform effective risk mitigation.

Question 2b. What are other areas that the Department sees as ripe for this kind of collaboration?

Answer. Today American adversaries exploit a fundamental asymmetry in our network infrastructure: While nearly all of our systems and networks are globally interconnected, our defensive capabilities are not. This gives the attackers an advantage as they can find and exploit the weak links in our systems from anywhere around the world—at machine speed. By sharing cyber threat indicators in near-real time, we reduce that asymmetry. As the President's Executive Order 13691 reflects, DHS and our partners are working together to find new and better ways to share accurate, timely data, including cyber threat indicators, in a manner consistent with fundamental American values of privacy, confidentiality, and civil liberties.

Question 3. Private industry and private researchers regularly make important cybersecurity discoveries such as software vulnerabilities or active malware campaigns. However, because even white hat security research often involves essentially "breaking in" to secure systems, some researchers are concerned that they could be subject to prosecution under anti-hacking statutes.

How can we ensure that needed security research is not chilled by these necessary laws?

Answer. The Department of Justice is best positioned to address questions specifically pertaining to the Computer Fraud and Abuse Act (CFAA), 18 U.S.C. § 1030. That criminal statute is part of a relevant exception to application of the Digital Millennium Copyright Act (DMCA), 17 U.S.C. §§ 512, 1201–05, 1301–1332, and 28 U.S.C. § 4001, specifically 17 U.S.C. 1201(g)(2).

The current statutory structure appears to be predicated upon the "white hat" researcher's gaining a copy of the protected copyrighted work after attempting to acquire or actually acquiring the permission of the owner of the data which is being protected by a cybersecurity system.

The cybersecurity research programs within the Science and Technology Directorate of the Department of Homeland Security complies with the CFAA and the DMCA its work to date has not been hampered by potential CFAA or DCMA liability. However, on occasion, DHS cybersecurity program officials have been informed by certain individuals performing academic research that their research has been limited by the refusal of certain entities using cybersecurity systems to permit research on the robustness of those systems.

The Department of Homeland Security believes that robust research is an important driver of improved public safety, security, and social progress and that the law must offer researchers the opportunity to carry out their research free from the fear of legal liability in the absence of being able to obtain permission.

Additionally, at the time the DMCA was designed, it was a commonly-held view that cybersecurity systems were in place to primarily protect against copyright violations. As our world becomes increasingly digitized, other areas such as protection of the electric grid, other infrastructure operational data, or, on an individual basis, research into the emerging area of cyber-physical systems or the "Internet of Things," which consists of research into the vulnerabilities of the increasing computerization of devices, such as automobiles and medical devices, can touch us increasingly both as a society and as individuals.

As a society, we must understand all such cybersecurity vulnerabilities, analyze the impact of the current law, particularly the DMCA and CFAA, and design a framework to assure an atmosphere that gives research the best chance to succeed while assuring the rights of the owners of the protected systems, the personally identifying information, and societal interests at stake.

○